# Mastering *the* Challenges *of* Leading **CHANGE**

# Mastering *the* Challenges *of* Leading

# CHANGE

## INSPIRE THE PEOPLE AND SUCCEED WHERE OTHERS FAIL

H. James Dallas

**WILEY**

Published by John Wiley & Sons, Inc., Hoboken, New Jersey.
Published simultaneously in Canada.

For general information on our other products and services or for technical support, please contact our Customer Care Department within the United States at (800) 762-2974, outside the United States at (317) 572-3993 or fax (317) 572-4002.

Wiley publishes in a variety of print and electronic formats and by print-on-demand. Some material included with standard print versions of this book may not be included in e-books or in print-on-demand. If this book refers to media such as a CD or DVD that is not included in the version you purchased, you may download this material at http://booksupport.wiley.com. For more information about Wiley products, visit www.wiley.com.

*Library of Congress Cataloging-in-Publication Data:*

Dallas, H. James, 1958-
  Mastering the challenges of leading change : inspire the people and succeed where others fail / H. James Dallas.
      pages cm
  Includes index.
  ISBN 978-1-119-10220-5 (cloth)
  ISBN 978-1-119-10223-6 (ePDF)
  ISBN 978-1-119-10221-2 (ePub)
  1. Organizational change—Management. 2. Leadership. I. Title.
  HD58.8.D337 2016
  658.4'092—dc23

                                                      2015022947

Cover Design: Paul McCarthy
Cover Image: istock / ©kyoshino

Printed in the United States of America

10  9  8  7  6  5  4  3  2  1

*For my wife Celest;*
*daughters Cherie, Angela, and Natalie;*
*and all of the outstanding people*
*who made a difference in my life*
*and the lives of others.*

# CONTENTS

# FOREWORD

Bill Hawkins
President and CEO, Immucor

S omeone once said, "When the rate of *external* change exceeds the rate of *internal* change, the end is in sight." That's a difficult reality for business today because the rate of external change in most industries is dizzyingly fast and accelerating still. Leaders need skills optimized to help people adapt, perform, and innovate in this turbulent environment.

Medtronic, the company where James Dallas and I worked together, operates in health care, by its nature a very dynamic environment. But there was probably no more dynamic period in the company's history than the period we worked together during which I was the CEO and James was the CIO. No situation could better prepare a leader to write a book on change, or even *the* book on change. James not only had a front-row seat, he was instrumental in helping us control our destiny and zig when everyone else was zagging.

Medtronic's culture is rooted in the five-point mission statement that our founder Earl Bakken wrote in 1960, focused on alleviating pain, restoring health, and extending life through innovative medical products. People's lives were dependent on our judgment, our actions, and our values. It was the mission that guided us to do the right thing every day, whether it meant suspending shipment of our number-one product when it fell short of our own performance expectations or increasing our investment in R&D when others were cutting back due to the economic downturn.

James was hired in 2006 to lead an initiative to implement a company-wide enterprise resource planning (ERP) system. This was technically challenging on its own, but it also required overcoming one of the company's biggest leadership challenges: how to align an enterprise that was made up of many distinct businesses. The company had gone through a significant acquisition spree in the late 1990s and early 2000s, and each business was protective of its autonomy. To succeed in his mandate, James had to obtain extraordinary commitment from a lot of different people, across multiple businesses and geographies, many of whom didn't initially see the value of having a unified system. Even among those who saw the value, there were many who doubted it could ever be successfully implemented. It was a huge leadership challenge, and even more so because he started out as an outsider—some guy from Atlanta. What we didn't anticipate was the economic downturn in 2008 or the uncertainty in our industry caused by the Affordable Care Act. As another former CEO of Medtronic and now a professor at Harvard, Bill George recently said, "Never waste a good crisis." James was not one to waste a crisis or to let external forces disrupt internal goals. He never wavered. He delivered.

When we interviewed James for Medtronic, I felt that he was the guy that you wanted to take a chance on. It was more than his track record. James was both confident and humble, he had a strong IQ and EQ, and he was authentic and principled—the guy you listen to when the stakes are high and the obstacles to change are great. Remarkably, the stories and lessons in this book help elucidate the actions and habits that add up to that level of executive presence, and the traits that allow for successful follow-through thereafter. Things like extraordinary transparency and disciplined execution, and the ability to recognize and groom talent and rally people to the finish line.

One of the recurring themes of the advice in this book is also one of the things I respected most about James: He never hesitated to roll his shirtsleeves up. Every quarter, at any public company, there's a big push to make sure you finish strong. The nature of our business meant that there were a lot of products that got shipped out in the last three or four days of the quarter. James would clear his calendar so that he could be on the ground in the distribution center or working with customer service until midnight when we closed the books. Seeing senior management right there on the floor, serving coffee or doughnuts or pizza, running interference or making decisions, made a huge difference for people. Because of James, they didn't mind working late.

That was something we had in common. We never expected anything of anybody that we didn't expect of ourselves. People felt that. They felt a sense of responsibility, or even of duty, to a senior leader who was willing to get in the trenches with them.

James is one of few change agents who has lived to tell the tale, and anyone who reads this book will benefit from his remarkable storytelling. On top of all this, it could be said that James epitomizes the American Dream. Relying only on the currency of principle, purpose, and ambition, he's an African-American man who went from nobody in Georgia to CIO of a major Fortune 500 company. Sadly it's almost uncommon these days to find people who have not only climbed the ladder from the bottom, but have done so with integrity as their primary strength.

James did exactly that. I hope his book guides many other change agents to lead their companies to greatly exceed the rate of external change—with the full weight of their character propelling them.

# ACKNOWLEDGMENTS

First, I'd like to acknowledge and thank my family, who have always believed in me: my wife Celest; daughters Cherie, Angela, and Natalie; mother Edna; father-in-law Carl Gibson II; mother-in-law Beverly; and siblings Deborah, Joe, Theresa, and Waymond. You all are my most important supporters.

Thank you to all those who have inspired, mentored, and sponsored me: my grandmother Momma Jessie, Gabe Lance, Al Jackson, Jim Bostic, Pete Correll, Lee Thomas, Pat Barnard, Earl Bakken, Bill Hawkins, Art Collins, Omar Ishrak, Gary Ellis, Janet Fiola, Carl Wilson, Mike Blackwell, Dave Peterson, Darrel Untereker, Mr. Prather, Coach Prichett, Coach Wall, and the Brimstone Consulting Group. Thanks also to the individuals whom I have mentored who are too numerous to name, but from whom I've learned more than they ever learned from me. Remember, never limit yourself.

Thank you to my best friends in the world: Gabe and Tina Lance, Alicia and Henry Reed, John and Carol Thompson, Bob and Jeanette Pfotenhauer, Jim and Edie Bostic, Selwyn and Janice Vickers, Greg and Debra Morrison, Bill and Susan Hawkins, Barb and Jim Szczech, Brian and Jeanette Ellis, Carlton and Shayla Weatherby, Gene and Elaine Norman, Jacob and Joyce Gayle, and Bob and Barbara Bostick.

Finally, thank you to all the people who contributed to this book, either by pushing me to write it or by helping me along the way: Jennifer Milch, Yvonne Bryant-Johnson, Vanessa McCants, Claire Derricho, Becky Blalock, Cindy Kent, Karen Murphy, and Sara Grace.

# INTRODUCTION: IT AIN'T EASY BEING GREEN

Very early in my career, when I was a fairly green project manager, I experienced an eye-opening defeat. I was leading my first major project for Georgia-Pacific in Atlanta. Georgia-Pacific primarily made building and paper products, but it shipped so much product that people often thought it was a trucking company. Shipping was our second-largest cost after wood fiber. My job was to streamline a freight-rating system that would process thousands of transactions a day across six building product businesses with over 100 manufacturing sites. I spent months analyzing the situation and gathering high-level requirements.

The day came for me to present my recommendation to the most powerful men in the company. I was more than nervous; I was uneasy. My presentation would define me for these men, to whom I was still an unknown. At the same time, I was confident in my recommendation. My team and I had figured out a way to standardize all the businesses onto one of the existing systems. This approach would save the company from an investment of millions of dollars and several years of development, and it required fewer people to support it.

I didn't have to wait long to wonder what they thought of my brilliant plan. Not five minutes into my presentation, I was interrupted by the most senior guy in the room. We'll call him David.

"This is the worst idea I've ever heard in my life," David spat out. My boss and my boss's boss were completely silent. So was I. I very quickly regained my composure, but it didn't matter. Before I left the room that day, a new project leader had been assigned.

The news spread quickly throughout the company. I went from being a highly regarded "up-and-comer" to the corporate equivalent of the guy no one would sit with in the high school cafeteria.

What I came to realize was that David and some of the other people in that room had already decided—before I walked into the room, even before I was assigned the project—that the *correct* recommendation was that we needed to develop a new system. It didn't matter how much sense my presentation made; as soon as they realized I was operating outside of their expectations, they stopped listening.

This was a powerful lesson in the politics of change. I realized then that creating impact requires a lot more than a good recommendation and the right job title. It requires you to be able to move others' minds from point A, a known, comfortable place, to point B, the great and threatening unknown.

I committed myself to figuring out how to manage those challenges. I would no longer first and foremost be a project manager; I'd become a change leader.

I started by taking some time to study change management as a whole and our department's track record in particular. I was stunned to find that 75 percent of recent, major change initiatives had failed to achieve their goals. Speaking now, after 25 years in organizational management, I am no longer stunned. I would say that's about average, whatever industry or department you're looking at. The pace of change has picked up dramatically, but the success rate has not. A recent McKinsey whitepaper puts the figure at 70 percent.[1]

As the years passed, I developed a comprehensive set of techniques and came to see successful change management being driven by four ⸺priorities, politics, people, and perseverance. Not coinciden-⸺ese are the four sections of this book. You'll find my focus is a little different from what you might have learned in a typical change management course. I took all those courses, too, and what they cover is important. But this is what I've learned as a practitioner, and it's not covered in the three Ts of project management: tasks, timing, and technologies. I've found that without these additional skills, everything else you learned is useless. (See my opening tale of woe.)

*Part I: Priorities* covers how to develop and launch a change initiative. By priorities, I don't just mean those you'll set for the organization. I mean those that already exist within the individuals and the cultural DNA of the organization. In this section, you'll learn a particular method of gathering data that leads to much more accurate insight; how to pick the core team; and finally, how to prioritize tasks to move forward quickly.

*Part II: Politics* covers the practice and theory of influence—how to build the alignment you need to persuade and motivate others. Politics are driven by the boundaries, both real and emotional, that give people their sense of safety, significance, and control. In this section, you'll learn why Captain Kirk should be your new role model, the best kind of messaging and the words to avoid at all costs, and, finally, techniques to overcome resistance to change.

*Part III: People* provides the insight into relationship building and human nature that you'll need to sustain and monitor progress along the way. You'll learn how to get to know people well enough that you understand their boundaries. You'll leave the section with a better understanding of how to build trust among your teams and a crash course in managing the group dynamics that can throw the best plan off course.

*Part IV: Perseverance* is all about how to fix the things that break along the way and how to create a newer, better way of doing things. Believe me, things break. Perseverance is also about how to institutionalize change and imbue it with purpose so that your efforts don't start with a bang and end with a whimper.

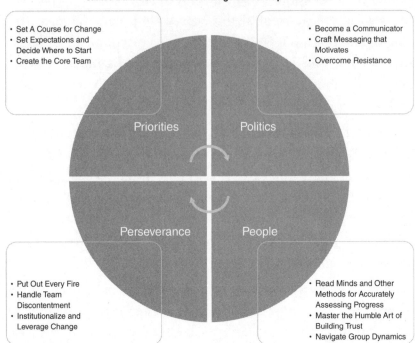

**James Dallas & Associates Change Leadership Framework**

- Set A Course for Change
- Set Expectations and Decide Where to Start
- Create the Core Team

- Become a Communicator
- Craft Messaging that Motivates
- Overcome Resistance

Priorities

Politics

Perseverance

People

- Put Out Every Fire
- Handle Team Discontentment
- Institutionalize and Leverage Change

- Read Minds and Other Methods for Accurately Assessing Progress
- Master the Humble Art of Building Trust
- Navigate Group Dynamics

Leading change isn't easy, as the meager success rate tells us. But what that means is that those few who master it find themselves in a tier above their competition. Their careers climb high and fast.

I am glad to say that my track record as a change leader ended up being quite a bit better than average. I was fortunate to work for two global, multibillion-dollar companies within different industries that grew significantly during my time with them. When I joined Georgia-Pacific in 1984, annual revenues were around $4 billion. They were just under $20 billion when I left 22 years later. When I joined Medtronic in 2006, revenues were around $10 billion. They grew to more than $18 billion in the seven-plus years I was with the company. My point here isn't that I created all that growth, but that the growth made the ability to lead change a job requirement.

At both companies, I brought people and processes together to leverage what was common and maximize what was unique. I led upward of 15 acquisition integrations, 10 enterprise resource planning (ERP) implementations, 10 shared services implementations, 5 quality and customer service improvement programs, and over 300 various other projects. I also created three innovation centers.

My track record in all those initiatives wasn't 100 percent, but I feel comfortable (if not exactly modest) putting it at 90 percent—not over my entire career, but certainly during the past 20 years after I had honed the methods I lay out in this book.

Throughout my career, I've paid attention to a powerful tutor called "trial and error," making a conscious effort to turn every misstep into a revelation. In my early days, that kept me busy. But once I got out of my head and shifted my attention to the people whose lives I'd be changing, leading came naturally.

We all come from unique circumstances that give us particular skills and abilities. I'm an African-American male who was born in 1958 in the South, raised by a mother and grandmother whose household was rich in wisdom (especially my grandmother's, as she told us often) but poor by traditional metrics. Speaking from where I am today, you could say I started beating the odds at a very young age.

As a kid I played the violin. In my neighborhood, that wasn't just unusual, it was freakish. I did it anyway. Being in orchestras led me to interact early on with people from other walks of life. Quickly I became a very astute observer of what made the people around me tick—an invaluable skill when you need to convince others to change their thinking when the status quo suits them just fine, thank you. So while most of the stories and tactics in the book come directly from my career, I've also included some "life stories" that I've found particularly instructive over the years.

The bottom line is that leading change isn't easy because it is not totally a science. That's why the failure rate is so high. Managing each initiative requires science *and* art, because the people dynamic is always unique. What I can promise is that you will increase your success rate by paying attention to those dynamics and respecting the "people" part of the equation. This book provides a wealth of tools to do exactly that.

Experience will still be your greatest teacher. I'm sharing mine to give you a jump-start and to let you know that you are not alone in the trials and travails you have experienced or will experience when leading change. Most important, I'm sharing them to let you know that the art can be learned and that you can overcome and benefit from any obstacle that you encounter.

## Note

1. Simon Blackburn, Sarah Ryerson, Leigh Weiss, Sarah Wilson, and Carter Wood "How Do I Implement Complex Change at Scale?," McKinsey & Company, May 2011. www.mckinsey.com.

# Part I
# Priorities

# 1 Set a Course for Change

I truly believe that the ultimate success or failure of any change initiative isn't decided along the way, but right at the outset. Unfortunately, most traditional project management methodologies set you up to fail. They almost invariably start with a focus on the problem statement. They teach you how to do the analytical work required to define the problem (a.k.a. opportunity). By analytical, I mean taking a structured approach to gathering the facts and making them as quantifiable as possible.

Of course, defining the problem is necessary, but the purely analytical approach ignores the most important data you'll need up front in order to succeed. Before you can set a course for change—in other words, set your priorities—you first need to understand the *existing* priorities of the people who you'll ask to change. That's the most important information you need to lead change successfully. Your priorities will never become their priorities without understanding their starting places, which is exactly why most change initiatives fail. Understanding others' priorities upfront—both their daily issues and the underlying cultural impulses of the organization—will help you craft a far more accurate problem statement.

It starts with a shift in perspective, which is the cognitive equivalent of a person taking his glasses off: get in close and rely on others to see. I started practicing this long before I wore a tie to work for the very simple reason that I was born nearsighted. I could only see in the radius of a few feet, and as a result I learned to use what *was* in focus to maximum advantage. For example, on the basketball court, I became hyperaware of what the other players around me were doing, a skill that made me MVP even though I could barely see beyond my own arm. (I never played in my glasses.) I could learn more about what was going to happen by watching the people than I could by watching the ball. I also realized that getting close to something—like the chalkboard, for example—was the best way to make sense of it.

So it goes with defining any new initiative. When you get started, go into the engagement with the attitude of a learner, not of an expert. Listen more than you talk. You'll get better answers and invest people right from the start. Once you understand what people's current priorities and practices are, you can begin to set a course to changing them.

## The Three Questions

A good friend always said to me, "Data is objective; however, the interpretation of that data is subjective." More specifically, people look at and interpret data through their own lenses, not yours, so your discovery process starts with them. Their *version* of the data is as important as the numbers or facts themselves. Therefore, the first data I gather when I come into a new situation is via a survey of everyone involved.

I ask the following three questions to my direct leadership team and to the key internal and external stakeholders, in particular customers, to whom we are providing services or products:

1. What are the top three things we are doing well?

2. What are the top three things we are doing badly?

3. What are the top three things we need to do to fix them?

The questions are simple on the surface, but they provide very powerful insight not only into the problem(s), but also into the existing priorities and how well the team is delivering on them. Note that I ask the questions in person instead of sending out a survey for people to complete. I center the discussion around a meal, and I go to them instead of having them come to me. This helps me get the best answers and starts building engagement early.

Often you'll find that by the team's own metrics, they're doing great. "Our success rate is 80 percent," they'll tell you. "We have a track record of finishing projects on time and on budget." But that's just part of the story. You get the other part by interviewing the clients or end users—enough of them so that you can spot outliers and see the pattern. Often, at that point, an entirely different story emerges. While a project may have been finished on time, it didn't meet the end user's needs. In the course of these surveys, you'll find out very quickly where there's alignment and where there isn't.

As you review and interpret answers from the team, you're getting a sense of the people and their individual priorities first. But you're also looking for a guide to the organization's practical problems. Primarily these will be:

- **Operational issues.** Are we having customer service issues, quality issues, supply chain issues, employee issues, regulatory issues, or ethical issues that are adversely affecting our customer relationships, employee relationships, brand, and so on?

- **Lags and shortfalls.** Are we behind on meeting the quarterly and annual budgets, behind time- or dollar-wise with key projects, behind on meeting regulatory commitments, and so on?

- **Strategic direction.** What ideas should we pursue, what impact could they have, what will success look like, and what might be the priorities, politics, and people dynamics involved?

Finally, your interviews will yield one more set of key data: team wins. Keep watch for what the team is truly doing well. You need to know so that you can leverage those strengths and also celebrate them. People feel much more positive about change when they know their value is recognized.

## Assessing the Culture

As you collect answers to the three questions, you'll begin to get a sense of the cultural impulses that are driving people's priorities. To change priorities, you have to change the culture. As the saying goes, "Culture eats strategy for lunch and new ideas are the appetizers." Organizational culture—the shared beliefs and behaviors—often cascades from the top down, so changing priorities usually starts at the leadership level.

Over the years, I have seen three typical cultures of dysfunction again and again when companies or teams within them are in trouble. Figure out which you're dealing with, and tailor action accordingly.

### The PowerPoint Mafia

In a PowerPoint mafia, executives and managers focus their time and attention on studies and assessments rather than concrete action. They aren't interested in changing because they think they're already the best. These folks love to hold meetings and prepare detailed slide presentations that lead nowhere. Indeed, their presentations are the best looking and best delivered you will ever see—in fact, that's often how they measure success. The top priorities here are short-term profitability and margins, even at the expense of growth. They are largely ignorant of (or closing their eyes to) changing market dynamics and customer needs.

The reason why I call them a mafia is that they are very skilled at taking anyone out who dares to question their way of life.

Indeed, many a change leader has gone the way of Jimmy Hoffa, never to be seen again, because he suggested changing priorities and doing things differently. Even worse, sometimes these organizations see their customers as the enemy. Executives at one company I observed suggested they should stop doing business with their biggest customer, an account worth nearly a billion dollars, because the customer was demanding (and honestly deserved) better value.

PowerPoint mafias tend to be large, previously successful organizations that are now stagnating or adrift. They are riding the wave of a previous innovation that has given the organization a dominant market position; however, growth has started to slow. When you survey people within the organization, you're likely to hear about how they are the industry leader, how profitable they are, and how good their products are. They are oblivious to or dismissive of their competition. They may have things to complain about internally, but when it comes to how to fix those things, they don't have much to say. They're also good at telling you why any given solution you might offer is bound to fail.

Customers of a PowerPoint mafia say things like, "hard to do business with," "slow to respond," or "provides solutions without understanding our problems." They're likely to be searching for alternatives, which can actually be a blessing because it can provide a needed wake-up call. This is true whether you're talking about a company or a specific service group within a company. For example, working with one corporate IT department, we thought we had standardized the company on a leading customer relationship management (CRM) package. In interviewing the internal clients, we found that we had over 30 instances of people "going rogue" and using another CRM program. Who could blame them? They told us they could install it more quickly and run it cheaper than we could at corporate. Overall, it was a better solution, and the CRM company was much more responsive to their needs than we were. That wake-up call was better than any speech I could make to convince people that we had work to do.

When dealing with this kind of culture, change agents need an external fire to light an internal one. Move too early and you'll find yourself in a bag in the river. Wait for those fires—loss of market share to competitors, clients jumping ship—and use them to shift the attitude of leadership. Only at that point will you have their full support and protection in changing priorities and processes.

This culture is in contrast to the next one, in which it takes a big internal fire to change the priorities.

## The Firehouse

Within this culture, employees know things are broken and that they are in trouble; however, everyone thinks it's someone else's fault. The top guys aren't leaders, they're firefighters. They don't even want to take the time to meet with you to answer the three questions. They're too busy firefighting—as they see it, heroically saving the organization again and again from the failures of others. You normally find this culture in mature industries or in departments that aren't high on the executive team's list of strategic priorities.

The top priority within this culture is—no surprise—putting out fires. They will recall with fondness the fires they have put out and how hard they worked to do so. They are proud that they are always ready to answer the call. Leaders in this culture can tell you things that need fixing, but the fixes are all tactical and generally related to the latest fire. Unlike the PowerPoint Mafia, they won't have any presentations or other analyses to show you because they don't have time to do studies. They don't want you to do studies, either—they want you to either put on your firefighter hat or cheer them on.

Customers usually have good things to say about a firefighter company because its leaders are very good at stopping flames before they reach customers. Actually, this culture is customer-focused to a fault. They have so customized their approach that they have fragmented, one-off processes, systems, and people (hence the fires).

The main problem with this culture is that growth stops because the underlying infrastructure, processes, and systems can't scale. Leaders resist "wasting" time on strategic planning and organizational alignment. Meanwhile, the front-line and middle management are desperately supporting broken systems and are on the defensive. They blame leadership and external factors and are worried that any change to the legacy system and processes will threaten their jobs and, more importantly, their hero status within the culture. They are firefighters, too.

Scratch the surface and what you often find is that strategic planning hasn't been a priority because leadership is lacking the skill set. Your first task is to join in the firefighting while you're figuring out who has the ability to help develop strategy and who doesn't. Your opportunity to shift priorities will come when a fire occurs that the team can't put out before it affects customers. At that point, the leadership will support you. Bring together the potential strategists you've already identified to develop a plan for change.

The saving grace of both the firehouse and the PowerPoint mafia is that leaders will respond to wake-up calls. Unfortunately, with the third and last culture, they just keep hitting the snooze button.

## The Thumb-Suckers

This is the worst-case organization for any agent of change. The thumb-suckers are disengaged and complacent. Problems exist and everyone knows it, but no one is looking to troubleshoot or improve things, though they'll tell you they're "working on it." If there's change, it's incremental and rarely focused where it's most needed. Business units in such an organization are typically siloed, failing to collaborate, and therefore oblivious to opportunities to improve and innovate. Their top priority is to stay under the radar screen of executive leadership. They resist direction and reject assistance. The front-line and middle management have given up because they feel their leadership has failed them and that they're powerless.

When asked about their company's decline, thumb-suckers show a victim mentality: Competitors aren't playing fair. Regulators have them hamstrung. Internally, they've been cast unfairly. They are helpless to improve, if they even admit there is room for improvement. Unlike the PowerPoint mafia, they are not at war with their customers or anyone because they don't have any fight left in them. They are beyond fighting fires because everything is burning. They're playing the waiting game, but they are on the defensive and therefore trust no one. That's why they only listen to each other.

Motivating thumb-suckers to change their priorities and to do the hard work of change is impossible. Don't even waste your time here; no amount of messaging will be heard. Your efforts will fall flat unless there's a complete change in leadership. Move on to an organization or division where you have some hope of progress.

The one good thing about this culture is that change in senior leadership has a major impact on front-line personnel and middle management. Suddenly, there's hope, and people are willing to roll up their sleeves and make the changes happen. However, until that point, change leaders need to focus their time somewhere else.

---

### Beware the Victim Mentality

Growing up in the inner city of Atlanta, my family didn't have much, but we never became victims. I give the credit to my mother and grandmother, who refused to let us feel sorry for ourselves. Our grandmother's favorite saying was "Keep on looking up." Their top priorities were those things that would improve our situation—moving to better neighborhoods, finding work, getting educated, and, most important, building a community with similar priorities. We didn't hang around with people who sat around complaining about how "the man" was holding them back.

It's because of the values my mother and grandmother instilled in me that if I ask someone "How are you doing?" and he responds by saying, "I'm getting by," I'm quick to say, "Hurry on up and get the hell on by me, because I'm getting ahead."

For the same reasons, I recommend that people hurry up and get the hell out of a thumb-sucking culture. If you stay in that environment, you'll get caught up in it. Leave, find an environment where you can make a difference, and then circle back around when the leadership changes so that you can then change the priorities.

## Ghosts, Hubs, and Mavericks

Once you've compiled all of the answers to the three questions and have a feel for what the current priorities and culture are, look for congruence in the various players' assessments of the problems. You may already have all the information you need to start working on a plan. But if things don't add up, the data-gathering process continues. It's time to move on to a second round of informal data collection focused on three sources.

### Ghosts

Ghosts are the previous studies and assessments of the problem that almost inevitably exist and can help direct your efforts. It used to b that the studies were easily found on the bookshelves or in the file cabinet of your predecessor. Now, you have to hunt down the digital files. I call these studies *ghosts* because the people who did them are normally gone from the organization; however, their spirits lurk in the reports they left behind. For example, when I first went to Medtronic, I found a study to consolidate data centers that had been done at least a year or two before I got there. The study's recommendation made sense; however, nothing had been done, and no one had mentioned it to me. I immediately put it on the short list of potential initiatives.

## Mavericks

Every organization has frustrated loners. Earl Bakken, the founder of Medtronic, introduced me to a certain category of frustrated loners that he called *mavericks*. These guys are super smart and see opportunities and problems before anyone else does. The problem is, mavericks don't communicate well and they often have abrasive personalities. They quickly get frustrated because they can't get anyone to see what they see. As a result, they think they're surrounded by idiots. In turn, the "idiots" reject or even ostracize them.

Unlike ghosts, which you have to seek out, mavericks will seek you out. Make sure that your gatekeeper doesn't "protect" you from them. I always meet with anyone who says, "I've got an idea I want to run by you," and the time is almost always well spent. Nevertheless, prepare yourself for some amount of ranting with those in the group, which will be repeated constantly if they don't see swift action. Your first instinct will be to dismiss them just as everyone else has. Instead, listen carefully. Between the expletives and the anger, you'll often find some good solid ideas about what needs improvement.

Remember the data center consolidation ghost study? It's not quite true that no one mentioned it—no one I *surveyed* mentioned it. But a maverick sought me out, and after a long tirade about the ineffectiveness of the previous and even the current leadership, and the need to breakdown the siloes in IT, he told me that I should consolidate the data centers. Not only would it save millions of dollars, he said, but it would also send a powerful message that we were going to start operating as a team. Then he looked me squarely in the eye and said, "Are you going to make a difference or are you just using this job as a stepping stone?"

Between the ghost and the maverick, I knew what needed to be done. Now I just needed to know why it had never happened, and how to approach it to get it done. Otherwise put, what priorities had averted consolidating it so far? For that kind of learning, I look to the hubs.

## Hubs

The hubs are the people in the organization that everyone respects and, most importantly, trusts. They are typically low-key, humble, middle managers who have been with the organization for more than 10 years. They usually have some type of technical expertise, which leads people to go to them to troubleshoot problems. Because they don't self-promote or seek out the spotlight, they often get overlooked for leadership positions; however, they lead through influence, not through title. Hubs aren't just sources of information; they're your most important partners in aligning people around new practices.

Hubs won't barge into your office like mavericks. You have to seek them out. Fortunately, they aren't hard to find because people will often say, "You need to talk to . . . ."

That's how I found the hub for the data center project. He was very polite in telling me why it hadn't been realized. The data centers were in several business units within the organization. Within each, people didn't trust the leaders at the corporate level to run a consolidated center in a cost-effective and efficient manner. The hub then told me what would need to change at corporate to make it work. It didn't take me long to find out that he and the people within the divisions were correct: No one within the corporate group was being held accountable for performance and costs. They had gotten very skilled at playing politics and being the "victims."

With changes made at the top, we were ready to shift priorities and develop a plan to consolidate.

## Wisdom from the Front Line

Don't make the mistake of only interviewing the people who think they're important—the executives and managers. As soon as possible, interact with the front line. See how they're doing their jobs and get their thoughts on what could be done better. It could be the source of a true breakthrough.

In the Introduction, I told you about making a recommendation at Georgia-Pacific (GP) that got me thrown off my first major project. I didn't tell you the whole story. That recommendation wasn't just my own; a front-line freight-rating clerk, Joyce, had actively advocated for it. She knew the system we already had could work because other large companies were successfully using it. She just needed my help to get all of the technical bugs out of the system to increase its accuracy and speed. She brought me up to speed quickly, introducing me to the companies that were making it work and to the software company's support team. She even taught me how to enter the rates into the system.

Thanks to Joyce's connections and training, I felt completely confident in my recommendation to work with the existing system. Anyway, as you know, it didn't go over well. I thought my career at GP was over. But after 45 days of doing middling tasks and looking for job opportunities outside of the company, I got a call. It was from the executive who called my recommendation the "worst ever." It seemed he had had a change of heart. He now wanted to promote me from IT project manager to managing the entire freight-rating process within his division, including all supporting IT. He said he was impressed by how I maintained my composure during the meeting! I was glad to learn that was the case; internally, I had been a wreck.

And so the transformation was on. We were successful in getting the system working for all of the divisions. At the same time, we implemented another small idea with incredible impact—and again, it had come from the front line. We received so many freight bills a day at GP that we had three people dedicated just to opening the bills and distributing them to more than 100 clerks for processing. Each division also had its own freight bill payment system. A payment clerk in our Crossett, Alaska, office had realized that instead of having the carriers bill us after delivery, we could use information already gathered at earlier stages of the shipping process to pay them automatically.

We called it "Autopay." Once consultants heard about what we were doing, they gave it a more complicated name: "Evaluated Receipts Payments." It was a great idea that never would have seen the light of day without listening to the front line. We were able to shift from needing 100 people to process payments to needing only 10, saving more than $10 million annually.

It was also the idea that put my career on the fast track. Within a couple of years, I became general manager of the Transportation Division. I eventually became CIO and an officer of the company.

Throughout this chapter I've focused on seeking out people and listening to their takes. You might be asking yourself, "How do I know that I'm talking to the right people and that they are giving me the right advice?" Here's my response: Talk to as many people as you can. If you hear the same things from ghosts, mavericks, hubs, the front line, and outside the company—including, if you're like me, from your grandmother—you can bet that you are on to something.

## Measure Leaders by Their Front-Line Relationships

Once you realize that the front line is a key partner in making improvements, another fact follows: Quality leaders cultivate good relationships with the front line. So, as you assess the performance of your leadership team and consider personnel changes, watch how they interact with the front line.

While running businesses and global operations within Georgia-Pacific and Medtronic, I always had the plant, distribution center, or functional leader give me a tour through his or her organization. The main reason was so that I could see how the leader interacted with people. If the manager avoided eye contact and didn't take a moment to ask about people's families or their days, I immediately knew we had an ineffective leader.

Once, while I was Medtronic's CIO, I was at a big annual event at one of our largest plants. Before the official program, there was a big "all hands" luncheon. I chose to sit at a table with front-line employees instead of with the executive team. (I always did.) I asked them my usual question: "What's the number one thing I could do to make things better for you?" I was sure they were going to say "more money," since we had frozen wages that year. What they said floored me:

"Can you get us better chairs to sit in?"

A lot of heads nodded.

"Ours are very worn and get very uncomfortable a couple hours into an eight hour shift." I immediately had them show me their chairs. The state they were in was appalling. Making matters worse, I knew that the same year, the plant had purchased the most state-of-the-art, ergonomically designed chairs—for the management team.

It was obvious that the plant manager had to go. The new one jumped on replacing the chairs. She was outstanding and responsive, and the plant's performance took a major step forward.

## The Importance of Looking Outward

Now, for another perspective shift: In setting a course for change, also look outside of your company, even outside of your industry, to get ideas and new perspectives. Now, expect to have people say, "But we are in a different industry, so what they are doing doesn't relate to us." I'm a big believer that all companies and industries go through the same cycles, just at different times. As a result, we can learn from each other.

Take, for example, customer care. At both GP and Medtronic, I always spent time with our customer care and service groups. I would put on the headsets and listen to them take calls from both customers and our field sales teams. Those calls and our care representatives' insights always let me know what was really going on with our customers, the quality of our services and the underlying systems and processes used to deliver them, and areas we could improve upon.

In our quest to have world-class customer service at Medtronic, we engaged a consultant who had worked with companies that were recognized globally for their service (e.g., Nordstrom, Amazon). We also visited several of those blue-ribbon companies. Drawing from those visits, our vice president and her team proposed that we develop a customer portal that would make us easier to do business with. Our representatives, field sales personnel, and customers would be able to use it to quickly access information regarding orders, products, complaints, and so on. (It may not sound groundbreaking now, but at the time, it was a huge leap in our industry.) We also took away insights on how to screen to find the best customer service employees—people who were built to go the distance to make a customer happy. We wouldn't have gotten those ideas without looking outward.

Another time we went all the way to Japan. As a company that prided itself on quality above all, we were constantly looking forward to improve. Toyota had just gone from being known for quality to being perceived as the worst automaker around, after a series of very public product recalls. To learn more about what happened, our quality VP, one of her direct reports, and I all went to Japan. We wanted straight talk that we could learn from, not any type of PR spin, so we met with people in middle management rather than the top brass.

They had two explanations for their decline that got us thinking. First, they told us that while their cars had become much more complicated—now more software than hardware—their design processes had not changed much over the years. Then they told us about a crucial step they had taken out of their design process. It used to be that their most expert and trusted designers served as a review team during various phases of the design process. They had taken this step out because they said that it had stopped providing as many recommendations for changes to the design. In retrospect, they found that project leaders, in preparation for the reviews, took a different look at their designs and made changes to them in advance.

That revelation made me think back to something someone told me about how people really come up with new ideas for problems they are trying to solve. Specifically, he said that people need to find a way to take a step back and look at the situation with a fresh mind. The review process had given them that step back. Needless to say, Toyota reimplemented it. We implemented a version of this review process ourselves, and it improved our process and products tremendously.

In addition to visiting Toyota, our research and development (R&D) people also visited companies within the aerospace, semiconductor, and defense industries to learn about the processes and methodologies they used to improve reliability of their products. Similar to Toyota, our products were becoming much more integrated and complicated. As a result of those visits, a company-wide initiative was launched to take our quality and reliability to the next level.

One of the most innovative projects I've been a part of was conceived by a marketing leader who was plucked from outside the corporate environment. This took place in GP's Packaging Division, which made boxes for other companies ranging from plain brown boxes to customized cereal, juice, and other consumer-products boxes. The leader had come to us from an experiential marketing agency, where he had designed and built the in-store experience for two major Nike outposts at a time when customers didn't have "experiences," they just went shopping. He had the brilliant idea to try something similar at a technical center in which our engineers had all of their PCs and machinery to develop and test new boxes. I was the CIO at the time, and he asked me to help him transform the technical center into an innovation center that we could open up to customers. The goal was to have a prototype of new boxes within an hour while the customer was still there. The rooms were designed so that the conceptual drawings that were put on the walls were transmitted to the computer-aided design (CAD) machines that were on the second floor.

Another section of the technical center was redesigned to look like a retail store so that the customer could see how the box would look on the shelf. A third section was designed to look like a warehouse so that the customer could see how efficiently the boxes would be packed, shipped, and unloaded. We had sensing technology throughout the three sections so that customers could visually track the product's movement.

The innovation center was a hit. The vast majority of customers who visited it signed contracts with us to make boxes for them. We later took what we learned and implemented an IT innovation that served as an internal showcase for technologies that could improve sales force effectiveness, supply chain efficiency, and manufacturing productivity. It too was a hit—and all thanks to the new perspective that came from a guy whose previous experience was marketing sneakers.

## The Value of Conviction

Many times, once you've gathered your data, both formal and informal, you'll be ready to make a recommendation. It'll be smart. It'll be innovative. You'll be on fire to take your company into the future. Then, you'll share that idea with your bosses and get a bucket of cold water on your head. They'll tell you it can never be done, or that it'll be too expensive, or—if you've got a real winner—that it's the "worst idea ever."

At that point, you'll need the courage to stick to it until you change their minds or can prove you're right. My best lesson in this came from my grandmother. During college, I lived at home and worked during my spring breaks. One morning, Momma Jessie (as we called her) pulled me aside while I was eating breakfast.

"James, take an umbrella to work because it's going to rain," she told me.

I couldn't recall hearing anything about rain, so I turned on the radio to check the forecast. I went back to my breakfast, and soon heard the click of the radio being turned off. I turned and saw my grandmother.

"James, come here, sit down, damn fool!" she said with emphasis. "Damn fool" is what she always called you when she was mad.

"What are they unlearning you in college? Are they only teaching you to believe what everyone else believes?" she said. "If so, you can bet that by the time you hear or see it, others will have already beat you to it. As a result, you will get, at best, a little of what others are getting."

She then looked me directly in the eyes and said, "True success comes to those who first feel things in their bones and hearts, and then pursue them with their brains, eyes, ears, arms, and legs." What a lesson.

hen grabbed an umbrella and went off to work. Everyone looked trangely because skies were clear and rain wasn't in the forecast.

Well, at about 3:00 P.M., the skies turned black and it started raining cats and dogs. Around 4:00, one of my coworkers came into work soaking wet.

I said, "What happened to you?" He responded, "It wasn't raining when I left home."

I then said, "Come here, sit down, damn fool!"

Once more: True success comes to those who first feel things in their bones and hearts, and then pursue them with their brains, eyes, ears, arms, and legs.

## Chapter 1 in Tweets

- Approach change leadership with the attitude of a learner, not of an expert.
- Data is objective; however, the interpretation of that data is subjective.
- Change leaders don't set priorities alone. They identify ghosts, hubs, and mavericks.
- Breakthrough ideas aren't determined by pay grade; they often come from the front line.
- Judge leaders by the way they interact with the front line.
- Look outside of your company, or even your industry, for a fresh take on how to do things better.
- Momma Jessie says: Feel things first in your bones and heart, and then pursue them with your brain, eyes, ears, arms, and legs.

## Coaching Moments

Make any question with a "no" answer your highest priority to complete within the next three months.

| Question | Answer (Yes or No) |
| --- | --- |
| 1. Have you personally interviewed a customer and a frontline employee within the past three months? | |
| 2. Have you done an assessment of the culture you are working within? | |
| 3. Have you met with a maverick or a hub within the past three months? | |
| 4. Have you gone on a best practices visit outside of your industry within the past six months? | |
| 5. Have you initiated any projects within the past year that represented a new way of doing things for your organization? | |

# 2 Create the Core Team

hen I look for leadership to helm a change project, I'm not really looking for hotshots. I'm not looking for average. Often what I'm looking for is the person who others think is a weak link.

Why? That's the person who has something to prove.

Earlier I told you how I was almost fired—and ultimately promoted—while on a freight-rating project at Georgia-Pacific. The story continues.

Being assigned to the project in the first place had been a crushing booby prize. Management had let it slip that all the A and B players in the company would, going forward, be working on projects to convert all of our IT systems to the latest state-of-the-art computer technology. Freight, meanwhile, would remain on the old mainframe. In other words, my assignment there was the signal that I wasn't considered the best or the brightest.

Still, I had faith in myself. Instead of accepting defeat, I threw myself at the project 100 percent. Ironically, the fact that it was still on the mainframe turned out not to be a booby prize at all. Because there was no new technology to learn, I focused on getting to know the people, and those relationships created the model for my success strategy going forward. I met with the key players using the system.

They taught me everything about transportation, rail, trucking, and freight, and I took the time to build relationships. Just as the project meant more to me than "a job," they meant more to me than "employees." Ultimately, we got the freight-rating system working, and my career shot forward as a result.

When it comes to picking team leaders, that guy that I was then is exactly who you're looking for: someone who views the change initiative as something more than just a project; someone who truly wants to make a difference; someone who has something to prove not just to others, but also to him- or herself. And if that person has passion but not the reputation or the title, all the better.

I've seen this kind of person succeed again and again. For example, when I came to Medtronic, my number-one priority was to get their global enterprise resource planning (ERP) project back on track. It was a $400 million project that was facing cost and time overruns more than double the original estimates. A common system had to be implemented to support the company's global growth, streamline operations, automate transactions, improve customer service and quality, and provide real-time reporting that would allow the business to make better decisions faster.

Many "high-potential" types gave me sensible descriptions of the problem and what needed to be done. I could have appointed any one of them as the leader and had management applaud my decision as unassailable. But instead, I gave it to an employee, Mike, who had in fact taken some of the flak for problems with the project so far. But he was the only person who stood up and said, "Let me lead this. I know how difficult it will be, but I also see how important it is to the success of the company. I want to make a difference." When he said that, I knew he was my guy.

Every time we had hiccups, I caught hell; there were times people questioned my judgment. We pressed forward, and ultimately we implemented the project on time and on budget. More importantly, the ERP system provided the foundation that then allowed us to reduce our cost of goods sold and our administrative cost by $1.5 billion, while improving our customer service. As for Mike, I promoted him to CIO when my own responsibilities expanded.

## Who's *Not* on the Team

There are a few employee types you can bypass right away. First, mavericks. Mavericks are typically creative and passionate, and they work better when there isn't a lot of structure. These qualities make them great at the research phase of R&D, but not so great at the development phase, which requires structure and standardization. Instead, I put mavericks to work exploring what our *next* change should be, and they're generally very satisfied with that.

Hubs aren't on your core team either. Does that surprise you? Hubs are effective because the people they work with trust them. Part of the reason for that trust is that hubs are within safe boundaries. People see them as "one of us" not "one of them."

Assigning a hub to the change initiative's core team would make the hub "one of them," eroding what makes him or her so influential. You're going to need that influence, so protect it. Situated outside the core, hubs can also keep the team updated on concerns that others won't voice. They'll relay the information circulating through informal channels (think *water cooler*, and all the discussion that happens once meetings are over), which can otherwise be hard to tap into. Finally, hubs provide objective and wise counsel when problems develop and tough decisions have to be made.

Finally, leave the tech zealots out of your core team. There is a difference between tech experts, who you need, and tech zealots. Zealots are so interested in the new technology in play that they lose sight of end goals. As a result, they often pick the technology tool without fully understanding the problem, or they overcomplicate the solution with way too many bells and whistles (i.e., "features"). They also tend to assume that their tech know-how trumps all, making them very disruptive.

I saw this in spades when I took over a wood procurement project at GP. The zealots running it were two years behind schedule to implement their shiny new technology system, and they were millions of dollars over budget. They had significantly overengineered things because they were more focused on the tech than on the results. The "Luddites" underneath them, people who were experts in the existing system, knew it. When I came on, they immediately suggested a solution that involved using the new technology on the front end and the old technology on the back end. The zealots were quick to reject the idea, but I was willing to give it a shot. It wasn't easy, but the team got it to work. We got back on schedule, implementing it at all of the sites. I'll never forget the sly smiles on their faces when we got the first site running. The cast-aside Luddites saved the day.

## The Two Questions That Count

An interview is like a first date: They're lying to you and you're lying to them, because no employee is that good and no company is that great. That's why as I'm doing interviews to build out my teams, there are only two things I ask to which I really pay attention to the answers:

**1.** Tell me the worst mistake you have ever made.

**2.** Tell me about the worst time you've been scapegoated.

Change is never easy. Indeed, the more transformational the change is, the more mistakes you and your team are going to make during the journey. And as change threatens people, the more unfair they're likely to play. Your team needs to be prepared for that.

I don't select people who dance around the question or give me
ll answers. I select people who are open and candid in telling me

about the mistakes they have made and the times they were treated unfairly. The winners' responses share one common theme: They never end with what went wrong. They end with what they learned and how they benefited from any given situation.

Mike, who you'll recall I picked for Medtronic's ERP implementation, had been extremely frank in telling me that he needed a chance to rebuild his reputation. He took responsibility for several mistakes, but he also told me about times he had been thrown under the bus—not to complain, but to point out where the real sources of problems had been ignored and to convince me that he could fix them.

In deciding whom to interview, I first look within the company before looking outside. I do this because people within the company will have a stronger drive to show what they can do and to be successful, especially if they have made mistakes or have been passed over before and they see an opportunity for redemption.

When screening resumes, I recommend a somewhat unorthodox approach. Rather than picking out the Ivy Leaguers, look instead for applicants who have something unusual in their professional or personal backgrounds that suggests they've had the experience of leaving their comfort zone: someone who grew up in one region of the country but went to college somewhere else; someone who got his undergraduate degree in English or history but is now in IT; someone who was a military brat who moved several times and speaks several languages.

I'm looking for people who have had the experience of being on the outside looking in. I've found that people with that profile are more adaptable, resilient, and empathetic. They have the ability to adjust to new cultures and boundaries, and they are more aware of how their behavior affects the team. I once heard of an elementary school teacher who gave her students a diagram of the classroom and an assignment to plot where everyone went to play during recess. The popular kids could only plot where they and their close friends played. Conversely, the shy, unpopular kids could plot where everyone went to play. They could do this because when you are "all alone in a crowded room," you see everything that goes on within that room.

In my case, I'm not looking for shy introverts, but for people who've had the experience of being different and the breadth of perspective it brings.

## Picking the Program Leader

Because all major change initiatives have many projects within them, a program management office (PMO) is needed to coordinate them. The PMO's leader is the second most critical role of the overall initiative. Don't try to have the overall change leader fill this role as well. In large initiatives, the leader has too much to do already.

Beyond that, the two roles require different skill sets. The change leader has to be skilled at setting the priorities, navigating the politics, engaging the people, and keeping the team together when times get tough; in short, the change leader needs to master the skills in this book. The program leader (PL) focuses on the tasks, timing, and technologies—they're still important. Not having a program leader is like not having an air traffic controller. There would be constant delays and crashes.

Good program leaders tend to be black-and-white thinkers. That ability keeps them focused on driving the project forward; you're either meeting deadlines or you're not. They're direct, straight shooters who want the same from others. This can lead to an office personality that's somewhat brusque and dry, even though I've found that outside of work, they can be very pleasant and engaging. Part of your job is to help manage the relationship between the program manager and the individual project team leaders. The PL will inevitably antagonize the team leaders at some point with rigid, inflexible thinking. Meanwhile, the project managers will try to defend drifting schedules and budgets.

You'll become the buffer, quickly stepping in and helping them reach consensus, then just as quickly stepping out.

A good PL will create detailed project and resource plans and identify constraints and potential conflicts. I attribute all of the success we had at both Medtronic and GP to also having great program leaders and PMO offices. I would never take on a large change initiative without one. They'll make you shake your head more than once during the initiative, but you will also shake their hands at the end because the team wouldn't have been successful without them.

Here are the traits to look for when selecting the program leader:

- During the interview, you'll hear things like, "What do you *actually* mean?" or "What are you really getting at?" because they want to be certain they're getting the unvarnished facts.
- They tend to be very solution focused: "Which hill do we climb?"
- They will be very specific in answers to questions. They never elaborate.
- Their postures tend to be rigid, as though they have been in the military. (Yes, really!)

## Two Key Roles That Are Too Often Ignored

I equate team dysfunction to hypertension: It's a silent killer that too often doesn't manifest itself until it is too late. The solution is to have someone who is checking your team's proverbial blood pressure regularly—someone with a human resource (HR) or organizational behavior background. For large change initiatives, especially transformational ones, this is a formal, full-time role on the core team because this person will keep his or her finger on the pulse of the human side of how the team is functioning, how the organization is functioning, and, most importantly, how you are functioning. Once this person creates trust, he'll be able to provide timely feedback and insight that will allow you to address questions before they become concerns and concerns before they become crises. The trust can't be created if the role is part time because the person would be dropping in and out instead of living with the team and getting to know them and you, the leader.

A good HR person will also help you identify and address nonperformers much more quickly than you could alone, because team members almost invariably know who isn't performing before leadership does. Indeed, it is very frustrating for teams when a member isn't pulling his or her weight or is a rotten apple; however, very rarely will the team go directly to the leader to complain because they don't want to be seen as ratting someone out. As they say, the higher up you go, the more people talk about you than to you. A good HR leader will erase this gap.

One final key role is a communications person. This is also a formal, full-time role. That's what it takes to get in deep enough to be effective—to understand the change initiative itself, as well as the existing priorities, culture, and politics that need to be taken into account when communicating. This person needs to come to know communication styles intimately in order to craft messaging that fits both you and the intended audience. This person will be watching both you and the audience when you are delivering your message. Over the course of the initiative, this person will save you more than once from sticking your foot in your mouth and slowing down the process.

The general manager of Medtronic's largest, most critical business at the time once caused a near HR meltdown that could have been avoided if he had been prepped by a communications expert. He was holding a town hall meeting to discuss some major organizational changes that were needed as the industry slumped. He had prepared his presentation well enough, but during the question-and-answer (Q&A) session, he was asked if there were going to be any layoffs. He danced around the question, and the room went silent. It wasn't because they didn't have anything to say; they were all expressing their anxiety and anger with their fingers, via internal social media. It became a productivity-sucking firestorm, and he had to call another town hall just to address the question directly.

Change leaders need communication and HR people on the core team that have their fingers on the pulse of the team, the organization, and you. They need to understand your strengths and weaknesses. For example, I like to use stories when I speak and need help in making sure that their points are clearly linked to the practical issues I'm addressing. Before any important presentation, I recommend a rehearsal that includes Q&A with a communications person, and preferably your HR person, too.

Too many times, because of budgetary reasons or because the leader tries to do too much himself, these two critical roles are either absent on the core team or are part-time positions. Don't make that huge mistake. The "people" part of change should be prioritized in your schedule and your budget, and it requires full-time help.

## Moving beyond "Off with Their Heads"

I've seen new leaders arrive on the scene with an "off with their heads" attitude that ultimately leads to unnecessary disruption and wasted resources. A better approach is to start with an open mind, prepared to listen. Evaluate everyone individually before making any personnel decisions.

Even when you're brought in for a radical initiative—or to rescue one that has gone into the ditch—very rarely do you have to replace everybody. Let's start with the leadership team. Yes, you almost always replace some, but not all. The senior people will each readily tell you what was wrong with the leader who was there before you, but only a few will be able to tell you what needs to be done to fix the problems. Those are the ones you keep.

Speaking more broadly, watch out for employees who, thanks to faulty leadership, have succumbed to a victim mentality—the thumb-suckers. These people no longer take accountability seriously. You may be able to reform them, but it will take focus and energy that might be better used elsewhere. In my experience, thumb-suckers have to go. I learned this the hard way during an acquisition integration. Everyone in the IT group of the company we were acquiring was a thumb-sucker. We did everything we could to reengage them, including giving them leadership roles during the integration. That backfired when a major system upgrade failed, and the team just pointed their fingers at the project leader, despite having recommended him in the first place. Meanwhile, they accused management of "never listening." I knew at that moment that this was one of the rare times the whole team had to go. Once we had new leadership in place, we successfully finished the integration, but I lost a lot of time by not removing the thumb-suckers immediately.

You can easily spot the thumb-suckers by asking people why an issue exists or a particular solution hasn't been tried. You won't hear "I tried and failed" or "I asked for the money and was denied." Instead you'll hear, "Because I knew they wouldn't do it," "because we didn't have the budget," or "because management won't listen to us."

At the end of the day, the people you keep are those who are willing to approach their jobs with a fundamentally different mind-set. Some will be, some won't, and how you approach the transition will determine the percentages in each column. In other words, leadership has to change its mind-set first.

One of our Medtronic projects completely transformed the requirements of our customer service call center. In the effort to make business easier for our customers, we had automated routine transactions through Internet and mobile applications. As a result, almost 100 percent of the calls the center was receiving were problem cases. That meant our front-line people had to be able to resolve the problems instead of escalating them and having someone else solve them. More important, they needed the mind-set of a nurse treating a patient in acute pain instead of an employee who was processing a transaction.

As leaders, we had to stop viewing customer care as an expense to minimize. It was now a core competency to maximize. We provided training, we created new success metrics, and we found new ways to recognize and reward stars. In short, we stopped treating the team as administrative personnel. By the end of the project, we had given everyone raises, and yet customer service cost less overall because we were able to meet demand with fewer employees. Customer satisfaction went from being less than three to almost five on a scale of one to five; employee turnover went from being over 25 percent to around 7 percent. Seventy percent of the original staff made the transition, and I've never been prouder of a team.

## Don't Partner with Cab Drivers

If you're in the business of change, third-party partners are inevitably in your future. The most important advice I can offer here is this: To maximize success, make sure the third party has some skin in the game.

I'm talking about shared risk. Most of the time, the software providers and consultants get paid regardless of whether the system works or whether the project comes in on time and on budget. Even worse, in some cases, it is to the third-party's *advantage* for the project to go over schedule because they can bill more hours. It's like getting lost while riding in a taxi: The driver wins, you lose.

Instead, build a close enough relationship with the most senior executive of the third party that he or she is willing to work out some type of risk-sharing agreement. You want more than a fixed-price bid, which doesn't work when the change is a high-risk one—in other words, when you're likely to get lost along the way. Penalty clauses within contracts are sometimes used to hedge the problem, but they're not all that effective. When things go wrong, everyone becomes more focused on placing blame than on solving the problems. This infighting becomes very public to key stakeholders and can cast doubt on the entire initiative.

The attitude you want to cultivate is that of true partnership. I once came onto a project in which this kind of infighting was preventing things from moving forward. I held a town hall meeting and surprised everyone by inviting the third-party executive to attend. I opened the meeting by saying that I was making two bets: one on the internal people on the team, and the other on the third party. Everyone in the room stopped looking at me and started looking at each other.

I told them we were in this together. Everyone's reputation was at stake. I then outlined what each party was bringing to the table and what we would do to become better coordinated and to build a trusting partnership. We stopped using the divisive language of *us* versus *them*. We started having group after-hours functions where people could really get to know each other. We also held weekly meetings with all leadership present. Ultimately, we became one team who were just on different payrolls, and we saw great success.

Whenever possible, give those tight-working relationships a head start by choosing third parties that you have worked with before. When you don't have that luxury, ask them to describe their last handful of engagements. If a company only references engagements in which the projects worked well, watch out. Just as with internal team members, I want to partner with companies whose people are open and candid about engagements that didn't go well. I want to hear what they learned from them and how they tried to fix what went wrong.

Finally, hold the third party to the same standards and values you hold the core team to. The third party has to see it as more than a revenue line item or a one-off engagement. For example, when we consolidated data centers at Medtronic, one of the centers had been outsourced to IBM, making them a key partner. The overall account executive knew that they would lose money once the consolidation was complete, but he was looking at the bigger picture. If IBM was successful in helping us consolidate, they might open doors to a much more extensive partnership between our two companies. When we ran into issues, IBM senior executives were in the war room with us. They brought in their best people—even someone from another continent when his expertise was needed—to troubleshoot. IBM didn't know what the future relationship held, but they viewed their role in the consolidation as an investment, not a one-off. That's the attitude you want.

## Team Diversity

Diversity on the core team is essential. I strongly advocate for building teams whose members not only look different but also, more importantly, think different. I once fell on my rear end because I failed to make sure a key team was cross functional.

We were implementing a new IT system. The launch deadline was approaching, and some critical reports hadn't been completed and tested yet. These reports would be used to determine total quarterly sales, which determined sales people's commissions. If we missed the deadline to implement the new system, our next opportunity was six months away. After a third-party audit and a lot of discussion, we made the call to launch on time. Well, sure enough, it came time to go live and the reporting piece still wasn't finished. Until we got things fixed, we endured, and rightfully so, the wrath of our affected colleagues.

The mistake wasn't in the call we made or even in the fact that the reporting didn't get finished. The mistake was that the team hadn't put a better contingency plan in place. They knew weeks in advance that they might not make the deadline; there was time to develop a better strategy. But groupthink had set in. Instead of telescoping back and figuring out how to change their approach, they just kept grinding. If I had put some hubs on the team from other parts of the division, they would have pushed the conversation toward new solutions. Instead, we saw a mess ahead of us on the sidewalk and kept going until we stepped in it while the rest of the company watched.

I never made that mistake again. Since then I have seen many breakthrough ideas that came from nontraditional team members. I remember one time in particular at Medtronic. We were driving a significant companywide cost-reduction initiative. I brought in Wendy, a woman from the facilities function of the company, to join the team. People raised their eyebrows, given that most of the members had accounting, process improvement, and program management backgrounds. One day we were discussing where our next round of reductions would come from, knowing full well that companywide, people were sick of being asked to cut costs.

Wendy piped up: What if instead of focusing directly on cost reduction, we focused on sustainability—reducing energy consumption, recycling, and so on? Great idea! We put it in motion and instead of getting complaints and low morale, we saw employees enthusiastically embrace the new initiative. We saved over $100 million in the process. It seems obvious enough, yet it was an approach we never would have considered without Wendy in the room.

Homogenous teams are fine when you're dealing with *problems,* which I define as situations with clear right and wrong answers.

*Data in, data out.* Problem is, when you're engaged in change—which in today's world we always are, whether we're in the middle of a formal initiative or not—you hardly ever have problems. Instead, you have *dilemma*s. With dilemmas, the potential answers seem infinite because the algebra of the space you're playing in hasn't yet been defined. Here diversity is extremely useful because, collectively, the team can evaluate the situation without the prejudice of the old algebra. Together they can come up with the *best* answer, if not the right answer.

## *Chapter 2 in Tweets*

- Select team leaders based on their passion for the project, not their reputation or title.
- Hire people who've been on the outside looking in: They are adaptable, resilient, and empathetic.
- Every project needs a program leader to track the details so that the change leader can rise above those details.
- Every change initiative needs dedicated HR and communications staff.
- Find ways to ensure that third-party partners have skin in the game.
- Build teams whose members not only look different, but also think different. Diversity matters.

## Coaching Moments

Any question with a "no" answer needs to be completed within the next 30 days.

| Question | Answer (Yes or No) |
| --- | --- |
| **1.** Have you determined why each person, especially the team leader, wants to be on the project? | |
| **2.** Are there HR and communications people on the core team? | |
| **3.** Has the HR person done a "pulse check" of the team within the past 60 days? | |
| **4.** Have you worked with the communications person to help you craft your messaging? | |
| **5.** If any third parties are working on the initiative, have you crafted the working relationship so that they have skin in the game? | |

# 3 Set Expectations and Decide Where to Start

Transformational change always involves uncharted territory. The end goal—the benefit that change will bring—serves as your North Star, but there are many unknown coordinates along the way. As a result, a change leader needs to be comfortable with getting lost. She needs to be able to get her bearings quickly, make the needed course corrections, get the team's buy-in, and then move everyone in that direction.

No one is more comfortable with getting lost than a nearsighted person with uncorrected vision, which, as I've mentioned, was me until age 16. I couldn't see signs until I got right up to them. When going somewhere new, I'd leave two hours early just in case I missed the bus or got on the wrong one. I carefully watched the people around me, and I was never shy about asking where I was, where we were going, and what the next stop was. When I did get lost, I didn't freak out, because it was already part of the plan. It happened a lot, and I knew how to deal with it. Little did I know I was building executive management skills.

But it can't only be *you* who's comfortable with getting lost. You have to prepare every other stakeholder for that moment as well. If your team isn't prepared, they're eventually going to be making decisions in a state of panic, or worse, ignoring problems and hiding them from leadership.

Your bosses need preparing. At the beginning of every change initiative, you, as the leader, have to give preliminary estimates on how long it will take and how much it will cost. I've found that regardless of how much you put caveats on the dollars and dates, the initial numbers are the ones executive management will remember. That's why it's absolutely critical that you set expectations around the probability of hitting those estimates.

Typical project management methodologies look to ease this uncertainty via "risk management." You're supposed to identify all of the potential risks up front, and then find ways to mitigate them. Sound nice, but guess what? It's impossible. The only thing you can control is how you, your team, and the executive management respond when the unexpected occurs, or when the expected occurs but differently than you anticipated. There *is no way* to identify and correctly assess all of the risks, especially with transformational change. There are too many unknowns. A traditional risk-management approach implies that you have your arms around the risks and have them under control. In other words, it sets exactly the wrong expectation.

A better approach is to make it clear to everyone up front that getting lost—losing control—is bound to happen. To ground everyone in this idea, I developed the Getting Lost with Confidence Matrix (see Figure 3.1). It helps people understand why we will get lost, the probability of it happening, and how we'll navigate our way back when the project loses its bearings.

H

| | |
|---|---|
| **4**<br>• Type of change: **Transitional**<br>• Difficulty to implement: Hard<br>• Politics: Hard<br>• Probability of getting lost: >50% | **1**<br>• Type of change: **Transformational**<br>• Difficulty to implement: Very hard<br>• Politics: Intense<br>• Probability of getting lost: 100% |
| **3**<br>• Type of change: **Incremental**<br>• Difficulty to implement: Low<br>• Politics: Low<br>• Probability of getting lost: <10% | **2**<br>• Type of change: **Conversional**<br>• Difficulty to implement: Hard<br>• Politics: High<br>• Probability of getting lost: >50% |

Degree of Culture Change (y axis, L to H)

L    **Degree of Infrastructure Change**    H

**Figure 3.1**   Getting Lost with Confidence Matrix: Factors and Probability.

## A Tour of the Matrix

The matrix identifies the two key factors—culture and infrastructure—that are involved in every change. Cultural changes are initiatives that affect the priorities, politics, and people within an organization. Infrastructure changes are those that affect the underlying processes and physical structures (buildings, factories, warehouses, data centers, computer systems, hardware, etc.) that provide the foundation for the culture.

The matrix shows the degree to which the culture (the $y$ axis) and the infrastructure (the $x$ axis) are affected based on the type of change. Where various initiatives sit on those axes tells us the type of change we're looking at and how likely it is we'll get lost. Understanding the type of change is not only important for setting expectations, but also for decision making—namely, where to start the process of change.

## Incremental Change

Let's start with the easiest change: incremental change, in quadrant 3. This type of change has little impact on the culture or infrastructure. These are tweaks and small enhancements, and these are the only types of changes you see in the three dysfunctional organizational cultures I described earlier: the PowerPoint mafia, the firehouse, and the thumb-suckers.

Quadrant 3 changes are all within the existing mental and physical walls of the organization, such as process improvement initiatives in which existing processes are streamlined. Because there are essentially no unknowns with this type of change, the probability of getting lost is very low, less than 10 percent. There's benefit to incremental change, but no sustainable competitive advantage. Polaroid is a great example: The company was attracting attention for their process improvement initiatives even as the company went south. The photography industry transformed, and Polaroid's incremental changes were not enough to save it.

## Transformational Change

Transformational changes fall in quadrant 1. This type of change is the direct opposite of incremental change. It involves significant changes to the culture and infrastructure. There are a lot of unknowns, and the probability of getting lost is 100 percent. Even with those odds, transformational change is worth the journey because it results in sustainable competitive advantage. Think of IBM and Xerox becoming service businesses, for example. Or think of Apple, Amazon, Quicken, and SalesForce.com, and the change they wrought on their entire industries.

While incremental change happens within existing walls, transformational change tears them down. Typically these changes make it easier for the company to connect with its customers, suppliers, and employees.

The politics of transformational change are dramatic because you're making fundamental changes to both culture and infrastructure. Silos are broken down and kingdoms fall with them. As a result, the "kings" resist or look to stop the change. Others may agree that transformational change is needed, but they disagree about how it should be done.

## Transitional Change

If we land in quadrant 4, we're looking at transitional change. This type of change sets the stage for a transformational change. It involves a significant degree of culture change but limited infrastructure change, reducing the probability of getting lost to 50 percent. Here you're breaking down the mental walls to prepare for the physical changes.

Earlier I told you about how we consolidated the data centers while I was at Medtronic. We started the process with a transitional change initiative by putting all the physical locations under one person (organizational change) and then by restructuring the employees' priorities and metrics, job grades, and levels.

The politics of transitional change are high because it alters power structures while creating broad change in people's job descriptions. Plus, people realize more restructuring is on the horizon and start resisting.

## Conversional Change

Initiatives that fall in quadrant 2 are conversional changes. Similar to transitional change, this type of change sets the stage for transformational change, in this case by changing the underlying infrastructure—tearing down the physical walls—while waiting on the culture changes. The probability of getting lost is again

50 percent, and politics are high because people recognize cultural change—reorganizations, downsizing, and more—is next.

## Figuring Out Where to Start

The probability of getting lost in any quadrant is directly correlated to the probability that your initial estimates of the time and dollars required to implement the change will be wrong. It is also directly correlated to the level of politics you will face. In other words, in a transformational change project, there's a 100 percent chance that your initial time and dollar estimates are wrong, and the resistance you'll face will be intense. How you launch the initiative will determine whether the politics and inevitable detours derail your efforts. That includes deciding where to start, who to partner with, how to fund the effort, and how to communicate it. It's not one size fits all; each type of change warrants its own approach.

***Starting a Transformational Initiative***   Again, this type of initiative is guaranteed to face intense politics along with detours from "the plan." For this reason, start small with a pilot site away from corporate headquarters. Headquarters is inevitably where the politics are the fiercest and have the most dedicated players. Choose a site that is as far away from you as possible. I'm not kidding about that—for example, when I introduced the idea of a central online customer service portal at Medtronic, we went all the way to Europe for our pilot. There was a very strong belief among the company's executive team that our products were too differentiated for such a plan to work. I couldn't change their minds regardless of how much analysis we did, so instead we found a testing ground in one of our European sites that was out of sight, out of mind, but significant enough that our results would be taken seriously.

Once you've chosen your pilot location, you'll need a partner. Find a hub at the site who has already identified the opportunity but hasn't had the resources (dollars or people) to do it. As I've said, don't put the hub on the core team; he or she is an informal partner whose influence will limit local resistance.

The next decision you'll make is how to fund the initiative. Don't ask either the local site or corporate. Use your own budget. This approach will keep the spotlight off what's happening until you are ready. If you have to use third parties or technology, find suppliers who will subsidize their participation in the initiative until it is successful. That's their skin in the game.

How you talk about the project will help keep the pressure off and the scrutiny low. Don't call it a project or a pilot; call it a proof of concept (POC). That lets people on the project know you don't have all of the answers and there will be a high learning curve. It also suggests that it doesn't cost much, so people are less likely to ask for the budget. Don't give the project a name and don't send out status reports—the goal is for it to slip under the radar of corporate. At the local site, hold weekly status meetings so that you can quickly discover when you are lost and make needed adjustments.

When your POC is successful, spread the word companywide, but make the hub and local site leaders the heroes, not you and your team. That lays the groundwork to scale the change across other locations because other leaders see you as less of a threat to their power or prestige.

If you're part of a mid-sized company, you may not have the luxury of a tucked-away site to launch a pilot. Here you need a different approach, as I did when I was asked to lead change within local sites at GP and Medtronic, which were run as individual profit centers. When a company is small, nothing you do can be low key or under the radar. Instead, run the idea by the most connected person in the company: the site's hub. (All companies, regardless of their size, have hubs.)

Remember, business owners are always looking for ways to grow their revenues, lower their cost, and improve their return on assets. The greater the potential impact of the idea, the greater the likelihood they will listen. The hub will give you great advice on how to position and communicate the idea in a way that will resonate with the leader. Try to think like the site's leader, who has to decide at any given time where to focus the company's priorities. Why should your idea be the winner? To answer that question, you have to project the potential financial gain. A hub is a great partner for that.

If you take it to the leader and he or she says "not now," recognize that small- and medium-sized companies have limited resources. Continue investigating to see if the idea could be tested at a lower cost or in a shorter time frame. And finally, don't hesitate to bring the idea back to the leader a second (or third or fourth) time. Your persistence adds weight to your idea and suggests that you have what it takes to see it through.

### BHAGs and Dallas Dollars

I'm constantly on the lookout for BHAGs: ideas that achieve big, hairy, audacious goals. These are usually ideas that make customers' lives easier and fundamentally improve the quality of our products, services, and people. In other words, these are ideas that imply transformational change. To sustain my interest, they also need to be scalable enough to accomplish one of three objectives: (1) increasing revenue to make a material impact on top-line growth; (2) reducing cost to make an impact on bottom-line profitability; or (3) increasing asset utilization to make a material impact on return on assets (ROA).

Whenever someone brought a BHAG idea to me, I always scheduled a second meeting with several colleagues to get their take. If they gave the thumbs up, I'd use my budget to get the idea off of the ground. At Medtronic, they started referring to this funding as "Dallas Dollars." In more than 20 years of allocating funds for BHAG experiments, I exceeded my department's budget only once. And it wasn't because of "Dallas Dollars," but because we decided to invest much more in cybersecurity than had been budgeted because the threat had ratcheted up so quickly.

---

**An Incremental Initiative**   Incremental change is low risk, with little political pressure. Therefore, you can start anywhere in the company, partner with anyone, and draw as much attention to it as you see fit. The most important departure in how you get an incremental change project up and running is in its funding: Do *not* fund it with your own budget. Have the person with the idea fund it or have him or her go to corporate to ask for the dollars; this type of project isn't that expensive and it's easy to make a case for because cost savings won't be far off. Spend your own budget on the three other types of initiatives since they position you to make real impact. If you have to use third parties or technology to make incremental change happen, pay them based on key deliverables being met. And again, once it's successfully implemented, you're not the hero; celebrate whoever had the idea.

**A Transitional Initiative**   Transitional initiatives should start at corporate. Because the cultural change will be significant, you want it to start at the top as an example for all to see. The politics will be fierce, but it is best to take it on early because ultimately this change will involve a major organizational restructuring.

Your partners in transitional change are the CEO, CFO, COO, and HR leader—again, the change needs to come from the top, and you'll need their authority to make it happen. Funding should come from the CFO, since the majority of it will be directed into severance pay when the company reorganizes.

Unlike with a transformation project, which starts with an almost "secret" pilot, here you want to turn the spotlight way up from the get-go. The entire organization should know how the company is changing. Hold town hall meetings and send out monthly status reports to the entire organization letting everyone know how things are progressing, including any adjustments made along the way. These initiatives don't need a project name so much as they need a defining slogan that focuses on the behavioral changes you want to institutionalize. For example, when I first became CIO at Georgia-Pacific, we launched a transitional initiative to tear down the silos between individual IT groups. The team referred to the effort as "One IT," and with that as our rallying cry, we got the corporate and functional groups to stop fighting and start working together.

***A Conversional Initiative***   Conversional change also starts at corporate. Again, the politics will be high, but it is best to take it on early given that you're launching a major physical restructuring, such as consolidating or outsourcing manufacturing sites, IT systems, or warehouses. Again, you'll need C-suite partners and funding from the CFO, because your own budget is unlikely to be significant enough to fund an infrastructure project. (For example, implementing an ERP system at Medtronic was almost a $400 million project.)

Again, communicate the changes broadly and frequently, through town hall meetings and monthly status reports. It's fine to give the project a name and announce start and end dates. Finally, make sure you have identified hubs anywhere the initiative touches. You'll need their practical knowledge and their influence to implement change on time and on budget.

## Plan for Change in Every Quadrant

The Getting Lost with Confidence Matrix is an important tool in kicking off any initiative—it reveals how you should approach the initiative and sets expectations with everyone else. But there's one more way to put the matrix to work. Good companies have a balance of the four kinds of initiatives, and the matrix can be useful in that, too. Executive management can plot all of the funded initiatives on the matrix. It will give them a good visual of how the company is being positioned for success. If all of the initiatives are in the incremental quadrant—which is exactly what you'll see in the broken company cultures I described earlier—the organization is resting on its past success. A painful wake-up call is in its future if leaders don't embrace more in-depth change now.

In the next part of the book, Politics, we'll learn how to deliver difficult messages effectively, so that priorities shift to creating healthy progress.

### Chapter 3 in Tweets

- Traditional risk management tells leaders you have everything under control. You don't.

- When leading transformational change, there's a 100 percent chance that your initial time and dollar estimates are wrong.

- Change leadership isn't one-size-fits-all; shape your approach to the type of change.

- Companies need both incremental change to improve existing processes and transformational change to blow them up and rebuild.

## Coaching Moments

All "no" answers need to be addressed.

| Question | Answer (Yes or No) |
|---|---|
| 1. Have you determined what type of change initiatives you are leading (e.g., transformational, incremental, etc.)? | |
| 2. Are the time and dollar contingencies you have built into the initiative(s) sufficient given the type of initiative? | |
| 3. Have you set the expectation with your team that there will be times in which you will get lost? | |
| 4. Have you plotted all of the initiatives under way within your organization to see if there is a balance among transformational, transitional, incremental, and conversional initiatives? | |
| 5. For transformational initiatives, have you developed a strategy for rollout, including partnering with key hubs to minimize the political friction? | |

# Part II
# Politics

# 4 Become a Communicator

All change is political because it inevitably redefines established boundaries. By *boundaries*, I mean the physical and mental spaces inside of which people experience the three things everyone wants: safety, significance, and control. Those boundaries could be practical or cultural. They could be a job description or hierarchy, the "tribe" of a particular workgroup or division, an office or seating arrangement, a title or a contractual agreement, a technology system, and on and on.

When you threaten boundaries, you face resistance—even revolt—unless and until you find a way to show people how their safety, significance, and control will be preserved in the new order. That is the true art of change politics: being able to communicate that you understand and will respect to the greatest degree possible the boundaries of the people for whom you're responsible. Get good at that and you'll find yourself more successful than not. Real success in politics, by the way, isn't just getting elected; it's using your platform to do something that makes a positive difference. For change agents, success isn't just getting the green light for your agenda, but actually bringing it to fruition and achieving the projected benefits for the organization.

Without effective communication, politics will bring an initiative to a screeching halt. I was once leading a project to install a chemical plant purchasing and maintenance system. The first installation in plant A had gone extremely well. We then went to plant B, which was almost identical to plant A in its layout, processes, and problems the system was going to address. I informed them, through a detail-heavy presentation, that we were going to duplicate everything we had done at plant A. I was very pleased with myself and expected that having succeeded once, this go-round would be smooth sailing.

About six weeks into the project, the plant's management called a meeting. The primary agenda item was my project. The plant's office manager had been assigned as the site leader for the project; she had the complete trust of the plant manager. Well, the office manager kicked off the meeting by launching into a laundry list of everything that was wrong with the project, including its leader (me!). She then recommended that we stop the project because it was interfering with more pressing priorities. ("More pressing priorities" usually just means "we don't want to do it.") I was completely stunned and, my confidence thrown, I awkwardly made the case again. No one was impressed, and we adjourned without resolution.

I drove the five hours back to corporate in a daze. I went in thinking I was these people's savior. I was going to fix everything! Instead they saw me as the great destroyer. After thinking about it all the way back, I realized that I hadn't taken any time at all to get to know anything about plant B. I assumed I knew it all from working with plant A. But people aren't plants, and I'd need the people's cooperation to change the plant. I needed to know the people.

I called the office manager the next day and set up a meeting. I started by acknowledging the arrogance of my approach. She quickly clued me in to where I had really gone wrong: The different plants in the division were constantly in competition. The people in each plant took pride in their respective operations. Their plant was their tribe—their boundary. By coming in and telling them we were going to carbon copy the work of another plant, I had walked all over the very thing that made them feel safe and significant. The last thing they wanted was to be "just like that other plant." I had also trampled their sense of control by riding in like I was General Patton, the conquering hero, and telling them what to do.

Because I hadn't taken time to understand the politics, I had insulted everyone I came into contact with. After apologizing again, I took some time to explain who I was and the reasons why the project was so important. Then I offered to remove myself from the project, if she thought it was best. She said she'd think about it.

They soon called another meeting of the plant's leaders. The office manager was again first on the agenda. She stood up and said, "Upon reflection and consideration of other priorities, we have decided that this project is priority one." She introduced me as "James, our project leader." This time when I got up, I didn't talk about the project. I talked about me. Specifically, what I had done wrong and how I needed to learn that lesson. The project went on to become a success.

One of the best ways to respect people's boundaries is to kick off with a collaborative approach. In other words, step off your high horse and learn from others first. (You've already seen this strategy at play as part of setting priorities in Part I.) I discovered this when I was put in charge of transportation at Georgia-Pacific. I knew the technology like the back of my hand, but I knew almost nothing about operations. That turned out to be to my benefit, since my first action was to have all the transportation leaders advise me on how to proceed. As a result, they had ownership in how we moved forward. We developed a collective strategy instead of a James strategy. Not only was it a better strategy than I could have developed on my own, but it was also one people were happy to implement.

## Never Soft-Pedal

Don't make the mistake of thinking that mastering political communication means becoming a master manipulator. You don't want to be Machiavelli, you want to be Ronald Reagan breaking bread with Gorbachev—*transcending* politics by understanding what's important to people and doing your honest best to respond to their needs. Never make promises you can't keep or spin things in a way that ignores the facts.

I learned never to soft-pedal from a hard-charging EVP from Arkansas named John. John had invited me to participate in a meeting around a topic that turned out to be very contentious. I was quiet until he asked me for my thoughts. Not wanting to offend anyone, I hemmed and hawed instead of taking a stand. When the meeting ended, John pulled me aside and said, "Never pull that $#@% again! I called you into the room for a reason. I wanted your point of view and instead you played it safe. How can I trust you if that's gonna be your MO?"

I realized then that you need to be *aware* of politics but not let them limit what you have to contribute. My motto became, "If you ask me for my thoughts, you'll get an honest answer. You may not agree with it, but you'll know you can trust it."

Even heightened sensitivity sometimes can't overcome the real problem: Redrawn boundaries create perceived winners and losers. Those people who were benefiting from the old way and are now handicapped by the new may never come around, no matter how hard you try to make a place for them. Some people will continue to fight the change by finding ways to delay it, disrupt it, and disparage it. Others will take the opposite route, actively seeking out the training and experience they need to adapt to new roles, processes, or systems. As a leader, your responsibility is to be as clear and transparent as you can, as soon as you can, so that people understand the changes that are coming. At that point, they can make their own choices to swim with the current or fight against it.

## Brush Up Your Speaking Skills

People who are great communicators understand and speak to people's boundaries. They understand what's important to every stakeholder. But "communicating" is the advanced skill. First you need to become a good speaker. When I started out, I mistakenly thought the most important communication skill in business was being able to give an effective presentation. I bought books and took presentation and design classes. Spinning globes, dancing babies, music—whatever you could think of, my presentations had it.

What a waste of time. Nobody listened to what I was saying because they were so busy watching my slides dance. Those who did listen heard me stiffly recite speeches that had been painful for me to write. Speaking in front of an audience terrified me. I'm the quiet one from a family of talkers. I remember a cousin once saying to me, "James, you're not like the rest of us, you hardly talk." I was ready with a quick comeback: "Hell, someone has to listen to all that junk you all are saying."

My first breakthrough came from taking a local continuing education course about becoming a better writer. On the first day, the instructor asked us to spend 20 minutes writing on a topic we were passionate about. We weren't supposed to edit or plan, just write whatever came out. Unlike when I sat down to write my speeches, I let the words flow naturally. My problem had been that I was overthinking each word and sentence. Thinking about it as a "speech" had made me so self-conscious I got stuck. That day in class, I just focused on what I wanted to communicate and let it all spill out. What I wrote wasn't perfect, but I could see right away how I would improve it later.

After class, I told the instructor how helpful the exercise had been. He told me then that the key to writing and speaking well is to simply be yourself. I asked, "That's all?" He said, "Yes." I then asked, "Do I have to pay for the entire course since I got what I needed and won't be coming back?"

Joking aside, I highly recommend classes to develop speaking and writing skills; they come naturally to very few people. Each year I took an executive media course with my direct reports during which we were filmed, got feedback, and improved our communication skills. I learned that people listen to less than 20 percent of what you say. What really influences their opinions is not what you say, but how you say it. Your voice, tone, and body language are the first steps in getting someone to listen, even if they're still wary of your message.

I also recommend reading at least one book each year on how to be a better communicator. One of the best is *Seeing Yourself as Others Do* by Carol Keers and Tom Mungavan. Put it on your reading list!

Here are a few other techniques I developed as my education continued:

- Never speak from a script; speak from an outline. The only time you should rely on a full speech or a teleprompter is when you're presenting on something very technical and can't miss a single critical point.

- Ask the audience a question every 10 to 15 minutes during your presentation. It keeps them engaged and gives you a chance to make sure you have closed the loop on key points.

- Never wing it completely. People can always tell. Winging it tells people you didn't care enough to prepare.

## Shift from Mr. Spock to Captain Kirk

My initial presentation at that chemical plant was the perfect example of failing as both a speaker *and* a communicator. I had thought my presentation was tremendous. It made a clear and highly analytical case for the new system, and I had moved through it confidently and at a good clip, my eyes rarely leaving my well-designed slides or the script I had written to explain them.

If I had paid more attention, I would have noticed the room was completely silent throughout the presentation. No one's heads were nodding. Later, I asked someone what he thought of the presentation. After a pause, he said, "It was very logical." In the moment I actually thought it was a compliment. Later I realized that what the guy meant was, "In theory it makes sense. But I can't relate to it or to you, and therefore I am not interested." The office manager confirmed it: I had come across as a pompous know-it-all. Hearing that hurt.

The bottom line is, you don't get anywhere by being Mr. Spock. There's a reason why Kirk, not Spock, was the captain of the U.S.S. *Enterprise*. People couldn't relate to him because logic was his only guide. (Naturally, he never got the girl, either.)

People make decisions not like Spock, but like Kirk: influenced by their emotions. That doesn't mean they're going totally on gut instinct or shooting from the hip. They look at facts, interpret them, and choose the path they're most comfortable with. Accordingly, effective communication requires not a recitation of facts, but speaking to what actually matters to your audience.

After the chemical plant disaster, it wasn't long before I had the chance to do it right. I had identified an opportunity to help one of our distribution centers grow and become more productive. It was already one of the most profitable in its division, in large part because the leader was extremely customer focused. His location served many of the prefab and mobile home manufacturers in the surrounding area, and he was constantly providing custom extras for them.

All that said, the center's order processing system was very old and was limiting growth. We had just successfully implemented a new system at one of our manufacturing locations in another division. Logic told me it would work at this distribution center as well. It was an obvious win.

When I flew out to meet the leader of the distribution center, I left my Spock ears in Atlanta. Our meeting started with me listening, hearing his thoughts about his business and what he needed in a new system that could support their growth. I told him about the system we had just implemented, but I didn't foist it on him. I suggested that he and his team evaluate it. If they thought it could work, we would support the implementation. He and his team looked at the system, and, even though some add-ons would have to be made, they were willing to go for it.

The fact was they probably could have found another system that was a better fit right out of the box. They decided to give this one a shot not only based on its merits but also because of the bigger picture of what I was offering: first, the opportunity to make the choice, and second, full control over the implementation with our support only when requested.

This gentleman and his team were accustomed to—and frustrated by—the corporate office dictating every technology decision. Autonomy mattered to him more than the specific technology, an emotional reality Mr. Spock would have missed. The leader and his team implemented the new system with responsive support from my people. At the launch party, he gave us a very heartfelt thank-you.

Well done, Captain Kirk.

## Talk Benefits, not Technology, with Executives

People are often frustrated with outside consultants because management listens more to them than to their own people. Indeed, the first step in almost every engagement is to hold internal workshops where consultants get the ideas of the company's internal people.

They then package them into a pretty PowerPoint and present the ideas to management.

I used to be frustrated, too, until I realized these people had a bankable skill that others, and especially technical people, lack: They know how to package information in a way that resonates with executives. (And they're definitely Kirks, not Spocks.) I started paying close attention to their presentations at senior-level meetings. I noticed these consultants, and the executives themselves, generally focused up front on the "why" before moving into the "how." As someone once said to me, "He that knows *how* will always have a job; he that knows *why* will always be the boss."

At the executive level, the details of a plan are less important than the impact you believe it will make. Presentations at this level should be weighted accordingly. Within the first minute of your presentation, hit on the benefits or impact of your plan, otherwise you lose their attention and your creditability. Keep the technical talk to a minimum. They don't care and they don't understand it. Worse, hitting them with jargon and detail can threaten executives' senses of safety, significance, and control all in one swoop.

The opposite applies when speaking to very technical audiences. First start with what process you used, the options you weighed, and the factors you considered in reaching your decision. Then, talk about the benefits. With technical people, you build creditability by showing how you reached your conclusion. They're not interested in hearing about benefits until they trust your expertise.

## When Not to "Keep It Real"

Have you ever watched Dave Chappelle's show? I often think about a segment called "When Keepin' It Real Goes Wrong." In the sketch, someone gets wronged and responds exactly how they feel, pulling no punches—and ends up getting in big trouble. It's funny and profane, but there's a lesson in it that applies to professional conflict: If "keepin' it real" means going off on someone, it is not the way to go. Authenticity in leadership, which is generally a good thing, hits its limit when it comes to losing your cool.

In political battles, some people won't play fair. Instead of debating you on the facts, they'll go after your character and try to paint a negative picture to others. Whatever you do, don't lose control. That's exactly what they're after, because your reaction will be watched and it will affect you more than their behavior ever could. There will be times that people legitimately infuriate you—when they have lied or treated you disrespectfully. Always maintain your dignity by keeping a level head; otherwise, you lose credibility. As they say, "No one listens to an angry man, even if he's right."

I once got taken off a project because I got angry. Really angry. I had been asked to audit a troubled initiative, and when the project leader found out, he jumped into damage control by hiring a consultant to do a separate audit and issue it before mine. The consultant never spoke to me, but in the audit he wrote that I had created problems. I was livid when I read his report. Madder than a hornet, I charged into the CIO's office, yelling that I wanted to sue the consultant.

The CIO knew that the audit was political foul play—but guess what? Instead of penalizing the project leader, he took *me* off the assignment, telling me I had lost my balance and needed to "go find my big boy pants." Keeping it real had gone very wrong.

Soon after, the project leader got a promotion. I was ready to go ballistic again, but the CIO told me to calm down. The guy had been promoted because he had some very influential supporters in the company—but a guy like that would eventually do something so egregious even his allies would back away, the CIO said. All I had to do was keep my cool and wait. And sure enough, three months later, the project leader behaved disgracefully in a meeting with senior leaders and was forced to "pursue other options" outside the company.

From this and a few other unfortunate episodes of keeping it real, here are the top things I've learned about communicating with difficult people:

- Bullies and bottom-feeders will eventually self-destruct. In the meantime, vent steam with someone safe (not your boss). Then, approach your boss calmly for advice on how to handle the situation. If both of you report to the same boss, ask another senior person who's in your corner how he or she thinks it should be handled. If you can keep your cool, you may be surprised to find that people will fight your battle for you.

- Never write an ugly e-mail to vent your frustrations. Use e-mail to congratulate or confirm, never to confront.

- Use a "block and bridge" technique when someone is inappropriate or disrespectful in a public setting. First, block by saying something like, "This isn't the place for that, but we can meet afterward to discuss it." Then, bridge back to the discussion at hand.

- If you are presenting material that is likely to be contentious, have someone prepared to "block and bridge" for you by asking another question to move the discussion forward.

- Ask a hub—someone who people trust—to address the allegations the person is making during workday conversations. There are times that your silence will in effect raise the volume of your critic, since this will be the only person being heard. Your hub is the answer.

## When to Tell Tales

Leaders have to touch both heads and hearts; you touch the heart and the head will follow. PowerPoint slides loaded with reasons touch the head; stories loaded with personal experiences touch the heart, achieving a much deeper level of communication. Stories motivate people to do their best and stay the course when things get rough, as they inevitably will when change is transformational.

The best leadership stories create a connection by meeting three requirements:

1. They clearly speak to the larger points you want to communicate.

2. They're authentic to your experience.

3. They are stories your audience can relate to through their own experiences.

When I was president of the lumber division of Georgia-Pacific, careful maintenance of our equipment and attention to rules were extremely important to keeping people safe. I wanted all of our employees to see that every single person makes a difference. So in town hall meetings at every single mill, I told a story about one of my first jobs. I was a janitor at the Pepperidge Farm plant in Aiken, South Carolina. My job was to clean the flour and dough out of the machines to keep the bugs away. It was tedious work. But Ernie, the plant manager, laid it out for me: If bugs got in, it would cause quality problems, leading to people not buying our products, resulting in the company losing money and people losing jobs. Ernie made me see that I wasn't just wiping down machines; I was a key part of the company's success. Knowing that, I did my job that much better, and the steak dinners Ernie served us when we aced our OSHA inspections didn't hurt either.

This was a true story that made my point while showing people where I came from. The story was very much a context they could relate to—they too were responsible for machines that required painstaking care. But what really worked was that it was easy for me to tell the story naturally, conveying authentic emotion, because the experience I was sharing really meant something to me. Decades later, I still missed those steak dinners with Ernie.

Someone once asked me what to do if you don't have relatable stories. First of all, I hope that's not true. It's hard for me to imagine that's true. We all have more in common than we think. But there's an easy solution if borrowing from your past doesn't feel authentic: Get new experiences. Visit their turf, do something that they value, interact with someone that they trust.

When I first started at Medtronic, a place with a very strong internal culture, I knew I'd need to be able to show that I understood what it meant to be an employee there. So I listened to customer calls; I travelled with field sales people; I sat in on every surgical procedure that involved our products; I visited plants and distribution centers. I also met with Medtronic's founder, Earl Bakken. By the time I had spent all that time in the trenches, I had plenty of material for stories.

With storytelling, as with any of the communication skills presented in this chapter, you will ultimately only succeed if you're able to develop content that shows you understand people's boundaries—what truly *matters* to people. That's the topic of the next chapter.

## Chapter 4 in Tweets

- Leaders need to channel Captain Kirk, not Mr. Spock.
- To change minds, shelve the tech talk and speak the language of executives: outcomes and benefits.
- "Keeping it real" has its limits: Never lose your cool.

*(continued)*

*(continued)*

- Tell stories to build an argument and a relationship at the same time.

- Public speaking skills aren't like riding a bike—you have to keep practicing to stay good.

## Coaching Moments

All "no" answers need to be addressed.

| Question | Answer (Yes or No) |
|---|---|
| **1.** Have you worked with a professional communications/media person in the past year to sharpen your communications skills? | |
| **2.** Are you viewed by others as an authentic, transparent leader? (Ask this question of your HR leader and have him or her ask it of others to see what they say.) | |
| **3.** Do you have a hub who keeps you updated when negative comments are gaining momentum on the grapevine? | |
| **4.** Do you have techniques to manage anger and other emotions when you need to rise above them? | |
| **5.** Have you learned how to effectively "block and bridge" to address negative comments in a way that quickly moves the conversation in a positive direction? | |

# 5 Craft Messaging That Motivates

**A**lmost all change management methodologies teach that messaging first begins with a leader's vision. He or she needs to communicate the vision. Vision is important, but this up-front emphasis on it creates a trap. You can become so impressed with your own words and ideas that you forget that your first job is to meet people where they are. You have to understand how people are feeling before you can create a shared vision. Feelings, not visions, are where communication and messaging begin. As I learned from my grandmother, "Feel it first in your heart, then pursue it with your mind." Once you create a shared feeling, you can begin to develop it into a shared mission and vision.

Remember first that what we think of as messaging—mantras, slogans, talking points, and so on—is only part of the story. A leader communicates nonverbally as well, through actions and behaviors. When I first joined Medtronic, people were wary. I was an outsider being asked to make big changes in a company with a well-defined culture and deep internal pride. My first task had to be building trust. Before I could talk about change, I needed to make it clear that I intended to become a real part of the team, not be the "hatchet guy" who zooms in and backs out just as quickly.

The message started with words. At our first town hall meeting, people asked if I was moving to Minnesota from Atlanta. I not only told them we had bought a house rather than leasing one, I also mentioned we had sold our home in "Hotlanta" and bought a snowblower and full wardrobes of winter clothes. These were all signs I wasn't blowing through town. I was committed. People's heads were nodding.

But it was my actions that really changed people's attitude toward me. I spent most of my first weeks on the job traveling to meet with the heads of every business unit in the company and their leadership teams. I attended surgeries so that I understood how everything we sold was used in the field. I was learning, but I was also sending a message with every meeting I took. My tour created a lot of buzz and won me the trust I needed to get to the real work of helping the organization increase its leadership position in a changing industry.

Finally, your behaviors send a message. This is the "how" in your actions. There are three behaviors that I believe every leader needs to model if he or she wants to be trusted and followed. First, be genuine. Don't act one way with executives and a different way with managers, the front line, and others. Second, be calm and level-headed. I always used to say, "Be cool, it's not brain surgery"—but then I joined Medtronic and in some cases it actually *was* brain surgery that our devices supported. Surgery or not, losing your cool is never okay. If anything, that's even more the case in emergencies and high-pressure situations.

Finally, be compassionate. Never forget that you're not just changing a company, you're pulling levers that affect people's daily lives; sometimes, you're messing with their paychecks. Change can be uncomfortable, and while you can't let that stop you, you can always be compassionate and respectful of the underlying feelings involved.

hese may or may not be the exact three behaviors you focus on.
's important is that you recognize that your actions and behaviors

are a core part of your messaging. You need to be intentional about them. In just about every company I've seen, the entire organization reflects the behavior of the people at the top. What you *do* matters as much or more than what you say.

## Become an Amateur Anthropologist

To create messaging that motivates, you need to study and incorporate the culture of your audience. I learned the secrets of workplace culture from a very successful change leader whose focus was acquisition integrations. Over 75 percent of them fail because integrating assets on paper is a lot easier than integrating working environments. Nevertheless, his integrations were always successful, and I'll tell you why: His degree wasn't in business. It was in anthropology. Thanks to that background, he understood how to identify and unify disparate cultures. That allowed him to turn two workforces into one smoothly functioning whole, again and again.

From him I learned that three critical aspects define a culture: language, heroes, and celebrations.

1. Language, both formal languages and local dialects (i.e., jargon), allows people to recognize each other as part of the same tribe and speeds mutual understanding and alignment. Industries have languages, but so do companies and functional groups within them.

2. Heroes are the people whose actions model the values and beliefs that are important to the culture. Heroes inspire others to want to be like them.

3. Celebrations are opportunities to reinforce shared values and strengthen community through ritual and relaxation.

If you want to learn a company's values, look to its heroes. Medtronic's "Superman," for example, is its founder, Earl Bakken.

He saved millions of lives by inventing and selling the external, battery-operated pacemaker. He is the most humble billionaire you will ever meet, soft-spoken and always insightful. His mantra for Medtronic was to focus on patients' care above all. And though he's been retired more than a decade now, that's still Medtronic's culture in a nutshell. Employees share pride in emphasizing mission above profit and making cutting-edge products that innovate medicine and save lives.

Given that culture, it was inevitable that they would be initially suspicious of a guy (me) who was specifically hired to cut costs. But because I took the time to learn and understand their values up front, I was able to show people right away that not only did I share those values, but also that the work I was doing would enable us to better deliver on them. Bakken himself saw the need for the change I was leading, and he embraced me immediately. Even in his 80s, and in declining health, he made two visits to headquarters each year.

As for celebrations, Medtronic's most important was the annual holiday party. It was attended in person or remotely by every employee. Every year, five or six patients were invited to come before the group to share how Medtronic's therapies had changed their lives. This annual ritual was so moving that there was rarely a dry eye in the place. The patients' experiences were being celebrated first and foremost, with the innovation of the devices that helped them close behind. Their stories were the living fulfillment of the company's mission statement: "Alleviate Pain, Restore Health, and Extend Life."

Of course, companies don't just have one culture. Just as people recognize and find safety within many different boundaries within a company, they create many different cultures. When leading companywide change, it becomes important to identify which language, heroes, and celebrations *cross* those boundaries. These are the keys to developing messaging that resonates broadly. At the same time, look for and respect the subcultures within the whole—plant A versus plant B, for example. Learn to speak their dialects and join their celebrations, and you will win a deeper level of trust than you ever could with one-size-fits-all messaging.

## Speak in Sync with Core Values

Underlying language, heroes, and celebrations are core values. To be effective, change messaging needs to support those values, or at least address them while introducing new values. That's how you show people that they're safe. While tasks, schedules, and roles may change, respecting people's values tells them that what's essential about their company and what makes their work meaningful will endure. When messaging matches their values, people are motivated. When the two are mismatched, fear escalates and people resist.

That explains why the messaging that I saw fly high at Georgia-Pacific crash-landed at Medtronic, despite having the exact same tagline.

George-Pacific had two core values. One was value itself—we prided ourselves on operating at the lowest cost. The other was safety. When I became CIO, I knew we needed to unify and streamline IT. As I mentioned before, the leadership team helped me develop the tagline "One IT," along with the mantra "Simplify, Standardize, Automate." Both the tagline and the mantra were very well received because they jived with people's desire to support the company by doing more with less.

Note that a successful mantra is more than just a few pretty words strung together. Done right, it conveys the essence of the change that's needed. Mantras are a simple but effective means of keeping desired behavior or process changes constantly top-of-mind. Moreover, repeating them to people creates a kind of linguistic shorthand to an entire change initiative.

Fast forward to Medtronic. As you now know, the company's core value is patient care: contributing to human welfare by alleviating pain, restoring health, and extending life. It is anchored on innovation. But at the time, the company desperately needed to cut costs and become more efficient. For several years running, expenses had grown faster than revenues. The CEO, one of the industry's most knowledge-able leaders, recognized this and knew change had to happen, and could happen, without sacrificing quality or innovation. The trouble was he launched his initiative with the slogan "One Medtronic."

This slogan cut against the culture in two ways. First, it screamed "standardization" to people, which they saw as the opposite of innovation—seemingly confirming the false notion that lowering costs means lowering quality. And second, it threatened the company's subcultures, which were its business units. The company had grown through acquisition and the business units took tremendous pride in their autonomy. This was obvious when I met with the business unit heads when I first started, and one by one they told me that they believed in "state's rights." It was their way of saying, "We are one when it comes to the mission, but individuals when it comes to how we achieve it" (i.e., "no way are we One Medtronic").

In the short term, people were unhappy and the dysfunction was high. And yet, it was a cultural change that needed to occur; in that sense, the mantra was the correct one. Ultimately, the initiative was a success. We reduced costs by 25 percent, or more than $1.5 billion. Moreover, the hard line taken by the CEO created room for his succes-sor to give the business unit heads more autonomy within the new uni-fied culture, get more buy-in, and reduce costs even further. Together, the two CEOs had delivered a one-two punch.

## What's in It for Them?

Slogans, heroes, values, celebrations—these high-minded aspects of messaging are all incredibly important drivers of behavior. But there's a more practical need that cannot be ignored: People need to understand how the coming change will impact their daily lives. Again, don't get so caught up in your big, bold vision that you forget to put yourself in their shoes.

I did that once. In the early 2000s, I traveled to India to visit several of the large IT consulting companies there. I was amazed by their operations. They had come so far so fast, having moved rapidly from year 2000 bug work to system support to new system programming, and at a much lower cost than we were doing it in the United States. The speed of Westernization in these businesses was equally astounding.

The visit was a major wake-up call for me. I knew our IT organization would have to change in order to be competitive. I was so on fire with ideas and urgency that I barely slept during the 20 hours of flight time to get home. When I landed in the States, I immediately drafted an e-mail to all of IT telling them what I'd seen. We would need to transform the way we worked in order to stay competitive, I wrote.

Now in my head, I had seen where things were going and was giving the team the thumbs-up that I was enthused and prepared to lead them into the future. I was sharing an *opportunity*. Well, that's not how the e-mail was received. They read it and concluded that I was going to outsource everything and put their jobs on the chopping block.

I had made a fatal error. I delivered the vision without also sharing the road map I had in mind. In this case, that road map was skills training in project management, system design, consulting, and leadership. Continuing education would make everyone in IT more valuable within the company and to the marketplace as a whole.

The storm my e-mail had created didn't dissipate until I brought everyone together and shared those details, which very clearly outlined the individual benefits wrapped up in the coming change.

Rest assured, I had a mantra that cut right to it: "Employed and Employable" was the phrase, removing the fear that their jobs were threatened while emphasizing the value of broadening their skill sets.

In that situation, I was fortunate in that I had time to develop the "what's in it for them" before I assembled the group. There will be times that you won't have that luxury. In fact, that's usually the case these days. In an era of global, 24-hour connectivity, news travels fast. Leaders sometimes think that if they wait to communicate until they have everything worked out, they'll ease the disruption and save people from worry. Since nothing goes viral faster than bad news, that never turns out to be the case; instead, employees get news that's often inaccurate, and they cease to trust the leaders who are keeping them from "the truth."

When you can't yet sketch out the future for people, do the next best thing: Make it clear that you will share everything you know as soon as you know it throughout the process. Acknowledge that something is going to happen. Give as many details as you can about the process to come, and always let them know when they'll get the next update. There were many times that I took this approach and found that people who weren't even in my organization were coming to my town hall meetings because their own leaders weren't communicating. Frequent communications help build trust and provide a sense of control. People may not know the future, but at least they know when they'll get their next update.

## Two Words to Avoid at All Costs

Language can have a powerful and immediate effect on people's emotions and, therefore, their gut responses to a change initiative. Leaders need to choose their words carefully. There are two words that I've found raise more fear (and stubborn intransigence) in the hearts of employees than any others. They are to be avoided at all costs at the outset of a new initiative. These words are *transformation* and *standardization*.

Executives and consultants love to use the word *transformation*. I guess it sounds glamorous and revolutionary and career-making to our ears. Unfortunately, it scares the hell out of middle management and front-line people, who will have to execute the transformation. Transforming is one thing; *being transformed* is another. That's how people hear it when it comes as a mandate from above. They think they're being transformed out of their jobs. Their security, significance, and control are jeopardized. As a result, they immediately go into defense mode and start thinking of rationales and ways to resist the change.

It's fine to use this word, but not until *after* you have taken the time to show what the change means to them—both their day-to-day concerns and their deeper values. At that point you can transform together.

The next word to avoid above all costs in initial messaging is *standardization*. People don't like the word because it diminishes their significance; they want to be unique and, therefore, irreplaceable. They also fear that their autonomy will be taken away because someone will be designing and controlling everything from afar.

I know what you're thinking: "Wait a minute! Wasn't 'Simplify, Standardize, and Automate' one of your successful mantras at GP?" Yes, it was, but before we used the mantra, we took the time to let people know exactly what was going to be standardized and what it meant for them. In sharing the details, we stripped the word of its negative connotation.

Now here's the bad news. There will be times that you've done everything right. Your messaging is perfectly in sync with the company's values, you've learned the local lingo, you've shared the road map, and you've even avoided the two danger words. And yet, some people still resist because they've been shown redrawn boundaries, and they don't like them. How to deal with these folks is the subject of the next chapter.

### *Chapter 5 in Tweets*

- Actions and behaviors speak louder than words; act with intention.

- Consider your audience's feelings first when crafting messaging, then start working in your vision.

- To understand a culture, get to know its language, heroes, and celebrations.

- People will embrace workplace change if you can show them that it supports their values.

- Want people to get on board with your plans? Let them know what's in it for them.

- Change agents strike *transformation* and *standardization* from their vocabularies until after buy-in.

## Coaching Moments

All "no" answers need to be addressed.

| Question | Answer (Yes or No) |
|---|---|
| **1.** Do the people who are being impacted by the change feel that you understand their values? (Have your HR or communications person ask people this question.) | |

| Question | Answer (Yes or No) |
| --- | --- |
| **2.** Are you addressing "what's in it for them?" in your messaging? | |
| **3.** Are you avoiding words that create fear, such as *transformation* and *standardization,* in your messaging? (Have an objective professional communicator review your messaging to determine this.) | |
| **4.** When uncertainty is unavoidable, are you communicating frequently and being clear about when people can expect the next update? | |

# 6  Overcoming Resistance

**M**y first week on the job as the CIO of Medtronic, I set into motion a change that, at first glance, seemed like an easy way to save the company a lot of money. Little did I know, I was kicking off the first scuffle in my dealings with a man—we'll call him Stymie Stan—who was determined to be my adversary. This would be the first of three times in my first 90 days that he would act unilaterally against a team decision. He was the worst, but he wasn't the only resistance I faced at Medtronic. All change leaders need to expect resistance—whether it be from individuals or entire business units—and be prepared to overcome it.

The trouble started when, the day I arrived at Medtronic, I sat down at my new desk and booted up my shiny, brand-new, company-issued PC. I was amazed: Here was the Maserati of computers. It was perfect for someone in R&D, engineering, or quantitative analysis who needed real horsepower. Trouble was, my top driving speeds, like most people in the company, would be e-mail, spreadsheets, and PowerPoint slides.

I asked around and found out that everyone in the company got the same computer. IT had set the standard based on the needs of the highest-end users, which comprised about 15 percent of the company.

Making matters worse, I found out we were paying through the nose for these machines. They were the same ones I had used at Georgia-Pacific, purchased from the same supplier for more than twice the cost.

After trying and failing to negotiate with the supplier, I raised the issue at my first council meeting. First I explained that 85 percent of the company could and should do their jobs with much less expensive computers. Then I suggested we put our business out for bids from new suppliers.

By this time I knew that this change, like any, would involve some politics: It would require the various business units (BUs) to give up some of their autonomy and align with each other and corporate over buying decisions. They were used to having total control over their equipment budgets, and they had tight relationships with the old supplier. This would be another step in the larger shift toward integrating IT services across the organization, a move that was already meeting resistance among the BU CIOs, who weren't used to having to take direction from the corporate CIO (me). As I've mentioned, the effort preceded me, but it was also a large part of my mandate.

Despite all that, at the council meeting my suggestions seemed welcomed. They all listened to my arguments, agreed that we should find a new supplier, and we adjourned. So you can imagine my frustration when I got word that Stan had placed a large order with the existing supplier at the same price we'd always paid. When I got him on the phone, he told me he had "changed his mind" about the need to find a new supplier. Although it was only Stan who had outright mutinied, the truth was many of the business unit CIOs were chafing against an initiative that they felt threatened their turf.

## The Many Faces of Resistance

As I've already written, people resist change that threatens their boundaries. Change can create generalized uncertainty, which no one likes, or it can create clear winners and losers. Guess who resists?

What's more unique is how people channel their opposition. Most folks take their responsibility toward the organization seriously. Still, they can be unconsciously influenced by their personal stake in the change, which affects how they interpret and prioritize the facts at hand. Their resistance takes the form of reasoned arguments and legitimate points of view. In my experience, I see four typical types of rational resisters:

1. Those who propose some alternative to your vision of the future (which often, but not always, conveniently preserves their boundaries).

2. Those who accept your vision but believe they have a better way of achieving it (see previous parenthetical).

3. Those who don't have their own solution but have legitimate arguments against the one you've proposed.

4. Those who have higher priorities and don't have the time or resources to invest in the change you are proposing.

I've found that people who fall into one of these categories are generally willing to engage with you. Either you can win them over to your point of view, or they'll help you find an even better solution, if you communicate successfully. Here's my strategic approach, broken into five principles, to working with dissenters rather than against them.

1. Drop the word *compromise* from your vocabulary. You're looking for *middle ground*. Compromise suggests that each party has to give up something. Middle ground suggests you're merely finding the place where your positions overlap and everyone's priorities are respected. The focus is on progress, not sacrifice.

2. Take the time to thoroughly understand alternative points of view. It shows respect, and in picking apart their positions, you'll either strengthen your rebuttal or find opportunities to strengthen your own vision with their suggestions.

3. Meet with influential objectors one-on-one to hear them out. It's very hard to find middle ground in group meetings. Work through the details one-on-one, then bring the result to your teams separately. Once that's done, the entire group can meet together for further discussion.

4. In your initial meetings, listen carefully for shared feelings and beliefs. If you can first get alignment on the "what," you'll have an easier time agreeing on middle ground concerning the "how," the "who," and the "when."

5. Don't try to rush to get to middle ground immediately. Spend time up front building relationships, preferably over meals. Wait until at least the third or fourth meeting before setting any timelines.

## The Fifth Type of Resister: The Machiavelli

Most people fight fair, focus on the facts, and can eventually be persuaded. But then there's the worst kind of resisters, the ones who are so driven by their need to preserve their control, status, and safety that they ignore reason and hold their ground by any means necessary. Determined to fight, they use dirty politics and ad hominem attacks to support a nakedly personal agenda. My adversary at Medtronic, at least at that time, was that kind of player.

I've found that no middle ground can be reached with this camp. Your goal is to contain, not convert. People who fall into this category should never, ever be underestimated. They are very skilled at politics, willfully deceptive, and experts at finding ways to attack your credibility.

Because they're experts at hiding their true agenda, they often at first seem like they're among the fair and rational. Even Stymie Stan kicked off his resistance to the changes at Medtronic with a detailed white paper arguing that diminishing the autonomy of the business units would have dire consequences for the company going forward.

Following are three stalling tactics that Machiavellis use to work against you, and solutions for dealing with each.

## The Rope-a-Dope

The boxer Muhammad Ali developed the rope-a-dope to defeat a much younger, larger, and stronger opponent, George Foreman. For most of the fight, Muhammad laid against the ropes while George whaled away at him. George wore himself out in the process, and after eight rounds, he was so tired that Muhammad knocked him out. In the corporate version of the rope-a-dope, you're asked to do analysis and more analysis until you just give up. I got rope-a-doped at the outset of the initiative to consolidate Medtronic's data centers. Some of the VPs ran their own data centers, and they wanted to keep things that way. They had fought the change by requesting study after study to refine the cost-savings projections. When they asked for an eighth study, I put my foot down.

"What percentage of the benefits are in question?" I asked them.

"Twenty percent," they told me.

"Alright then, let's start consolidating and get that 80 percent that you feel sure about—and then do a separate analysis on the remaining 20 percent."

They were ticked, but what could they say? We started the process by working with the business units that supported the consolidation and circled back once success was inarguable.

If you find yourself up against the ropes, ask for clarity: Exactly what aspects of the existing study are questionable? Send a team to walk the resisters through it, point by point. If they still are unsatisfied, find a way to move forward anyway. Start in an area that doesn't require their approval. Acknowledge their concerns, but let them know that you're getting started where the costs and benefits are clear. Whatever you do, don't get trapped into another study.

## The Moonwalk

Remember Michael Jackson's signature move? The person doing this dance is making all the motions of moving forward, and yet glides backward. You'll see this with people resisting change, too. They nod and say yes and go through all the motions of supporting your efforts, but they're not your allies. For example, you meet with "Bob" several times and he gives you the strong impression that he's with you. Soon you're in a meeting to win more people over to your initiative. You turn to Bob and say, "Hey, tell them all about how things are going to be better." You hear silence. You then again say, "Bob?" The next thing you know, Bob has left the building. He's moonwalked on you.

The way to protect yourself from moonwalkers is to get people to give you their thoughts in writing whenever possible. It's easy enough to do. After a meeting, outline their response in an e-mail, saying, "I'd like to confirm what I thought I heard during our conversation, and lay out the next steps."

If you can't get the person to commit in writing, or if the answer is that you misunderstood, don't panic or get frustrated. Apologize for getting it wrong and suggest another meeting to clarify it. In other words, block and bridge.

## Friday the 13th

In every single movie in the Friday the 13th franchise, the heroes think they've killed the villain, Jason, and then Jason comes back to life to terrorize them once more. Likewise, resisters will find some past issue they can use to put you on the defensive and shake people's confidence in your leadership. And every time you think you've put it to rest, they'll trot it out again, like Jason surging out of the lake. You're forced to spend more time explaining and selling, instead of moving forward and making things happen.

At Medtronic, "Jason" came in the form of a bad decision I made when transitioning our field sales group to smartphones. The plan was good: Smartphones would allow sales reps to access customer, product, and shipment information instantly without having to call customer care. In certain markets reps were already using the phones, and everything was working great. Very sure of ourselves, we picked a name-brand provider and rolled the phones out nationally. Very quickly we were in crisis: the phones worked fine in some regions, but in others they dropped calls right and left. Both the reps and the customers were furious. It was a huge mess. We resolved it quickly by changing phones and providers, but it didn't matter. Every time we announced a new initiative, resisters brought up the phone debacle as a way to question my judgment.

The way forward in such a scenario is via the block and bridge technique I introduced earlier. First, acknowledge and take accountability for what happened (i.e., block), then bridge into the lessons you learned, how those lessons have been applied successfully since, and how they will be applied again with this new initiative. When an opponent to change brought up the phones, I'd say to him or her, "Yes, that was then." Then I'd bridge by shifting my gaze to everyone else in the room/audience and saying, "What do you think of the new phones and applications that are on them?" Everyone in the room would give a thumbs-up, since the crisis was in fact long past. I'd then mention that as new applications were being introduced, they were tested by people in every region: "Once they give us the thumbs-up, we start rolling it out to everyone." I ended by pointing out two sales people in the room who could answer any further questions about the testing and the benefits of the new applications. By shifting the conversation to the present and future, and my attention to the entire room, I essentially confined Jason to the past.

Sometimes, you might find someone isn't just rehashing your mistakes, but embellishing them to make you look bad. When that happens, stay calm. Don't get defensive or call them liars. Instead say, "I really learned from that, and let me tell you how." Use that introduction to tell the story exactly as it happened, correcting the facts without calling the other person out.

## Removing a Toxic Player

To protect their agendas, Machiavellis will often resort to personal attacks on your credibility, particularly if you are moving forward despite their efforts to stymie change. For me, that's often the point where I stop trying to manage the person and instead find a way to remove him because he is toxic to the progress.

That's where things landed with Stymie Stan. After I interceded to make a decision in the case of the two technology suppliers, he wrote me an e-mail accusing me of taking a bribe from the winning supplier. It was a direct attack on my character and integrity. It confirmed that he would do whatever it took to continue operating in a silo instead of being part of the overall team. Ironically, he could have been a very effective leader for the company as a whole, and potentially the next CIO, if he thought broader and was able to wear both his BU hat and the enterprise one.

When dealing with a toxic adversary, protect yourself. First, build a coalition of hubs. They will speak for you when you are not in the room. Nothing is more powerful than having someone who is respected come to your defense. The hubs will neutralize people with personal agendas faster and more effectively than you ever could, because no one questions their motives.

Second, keep your ear to the grapevine. If adversaries are making personal attacks to your face, you can bet they're repeating them to others behind your back as well. Develop your defense so that you can respond quickly and effectively when you hear that negative gossip is circulating. Timing is key: If you wait too long, the rumors and personal attacks will get stronger in the retelling, and the lack of rebuttal from you or others will seem to confirm them.

Once you have support, you can make a resource change. When it came to Stan, I first met with Medtronic's CFO and a top HR person, both of whom were hubs and people whose advice I valued and trusted. I then met with the CEO and COO. Finally, I met with the senior vice president of the business unit Stan was in. All understood and supported the decision I made to remove him from the team.

I didn't fire Stan; I removed him from his IT leadership position and the IT organization. The BU he was in gave him another, much smaller position in the business. He left the company within a year. I strongly believe that he learned from the experience, because I heard reports that he improved his leadership style considerably after he left.

## Cleaning Up the Sludge

Firing or demoting someone requires a thoughtful and proactive communication strategy to move forward. You may understand why the person had to go, but it may not be immediately clear to the people he managed; they're still stuck in the toxic sludge. Stan, for example, was an extremely popular leader within his business unit. Once again, it's your job to help people understand how things will change—or otherwise put, to help people rebuild their boundaries. Start with these three steps:

**1.** *Identify interim leadership.* Name the interim leader at the same time you transition the person out. You can't afford a void in leadership while you search for the permanent replacement. Don't act as the interim leader yourself; you can't run the person's group and also lead the entire organization. Choose someone who reported to the person who was removed and who is trusted by her team. When prepping the interim leader, don't talk about the specifics that led to the change if they are behavior related. As the leader, you have to operate in confidence and keep the personal out of the discussion, even when others don't.

**2.** *Announce the transition.* Within an hour of informing the transitioning parties, hold a town hall meeting with everyone who works under the interim leader. News will spread even faster than an hour, so don't wait. Expect people loyal to the removed person to be frustrated, angry, and confused. They've likely heard a very one-sided version of the story. After announcing the transition, your focus will be on the future. Instead of talking about the reasons the change was made—remember, you're not going there—instead let people know the direction the organization is headed in. Emphasize the core behaviors that should guide everyone in the organization, including their new leader.

Don't be surprised if a person or two crosses the line with his or her comments and becomes disrespectful. Have HR in the room to address such comments. Don't ask the interim leader to speak. You want people to direct their frustration at you, not at the new leader. You don't want the new leader perceived as a traitor. Let everyone know what the process and timing will be to select a permanent leader.

**3.** *Stay positive while the hubs whisper.* After the meeting, let your presence be known by visiting the person's site often and walking through it. Meanwhile, let your hubs work the informal channels. They can say what you can't. They'll know the full story not because you told them, but because they are so well connected. Hubs know organizational history, including who the office bullies are. Chances are you're not the first person who has incurred a bully's wrath. Led by hubs, the water-cooler and grapevine talk will quickly change from how you did the person wrong to what the person did wrong—not only to you but to others in the past.

As for you, you'll keep it positive. Everyone will respect you for communicating proactively at the town hall meetings and taking the high road and not getting into the personal specifics. That's what leaders do. In a month or so, the toxic sludge will subside. By the time you select and announce the permanent leader, the halls will be clear.

That's exactly what happened at Medtronic. Ultimately, we got our new computers and the supplier offered prices even lower than what I had paid at Georgia-Pacific; this was a huge win that I was able to credit to the people who managed the bidding process, making them the heroes.

Those computers were an important win beyond the cost savings. Now even the most skeptical of people were becoming believers that quality and low cost weren't mutually exclusive.

## Influencing the Narrative on the Front Line

Front-line personnel are what I call the "last mile" of change initiatives, where the rubber meets the road. They're the ones making the products, shipping them, accepting payments, and interacting with customers. If they don't adopt the new processes and behaviors you're leading, the disorder tends to land directly in the customer's lap.

Consequently, it is very important that the leader keeps his finger on the pulse of how personnel are feeling and what they are saying, stepping in when necessary to influence the narrative. These days, information readily flows up and down, especially in this age of social media, in which remarks—both positive and negative—can go viral in an instant. Controlling messaging is impossible, so exactly how *do* you influence the narrative? No amount of propaganda will silence the rank and file, who have no reason not to tell it like they see it. Given that, I suggest you do the exact opposite. Instead of trying to talk louder, I want you to *listen*.

Go to the places where the front line works and hold listening sessions, both in groups and one-on-one. By spending time with people, you will learn how they feel. You'll get valuable information and be able to discuss their concerns directly. But again, you're mostly listening; they're the ones who will influence the narrative. While you're visiting they're not only talking to you; they're also texting, posting status updates, and tagging photos, letting others know that you are there with them. The message to everyone is loud and clear: You care about what they have to say and how they are being effected. Their leaders are listening. That's a message you *want* to go viral.

Listening to the front line has an additional benefit: You'll emerge from these interactions with some close relationships. Those people become your communications front line, shooting you texts if they see issues or resistance as the changes unroll. You'll be able to troubleshoot quickly, before problems hit the customer or negative information flows up to the top.

## Information Flows Up

Receptionists and security guards can be incredibly valuable sources of information if you take the time to have good relationships with them. They are practical hubs, well positioned to observe everything that's going on. They are very perceptive, and with that broad view, they can connect dots faster than anyone. They can give you a heads up such as, "I saw so-and-so in the building today."

Take the time to build relationships with these people. Greet them in the mornings and say good-bye in the evenings. Find out what's important to them, professionally and personally. And if they ever ask, "How is everything going for you?" stop dead in your tracks. That question often means that they heard something negative, so listen carefully.

Visiting the front line becomes increasingly difficult as you move up the ladder. It takes time to interact in person, and the higher up you go, the more crowded your schedule gets with meetings in the corporate headquarters. You'll need to prioritize in order to make front-line visits possible. Enlist your executive assistant to help. Mine used to schedule "walk around" time for me several hours each week. Those times consisted of me just walking around the campus, chatting people up. I always learned a lot that way. In scheduled meetings, people have rehearsed and are on their guard to say things in the most politically correct way. When you can catch them on the way to the restroom, the information you get is candid—and incredibly succinct.

Of course, the information you get is only as good as the relationships you have. Part III, People, is all about how to make your relationships stronger.

## Chapter 6 in Tweets

- Engage people who oppose change with rational arguments; they may improve your plan.

- Don't let your change initiative get stuck in another study. Start small and show results.

- Get people's positions in writing to protect yourself from moonwalkers.

- When people fight change with personal attacks, the best use of your energy is to let the attacks go.

- Don't wait to announce a personnel change; you've got an hour before the grapevine does the job for you.

- Spending time with the front line creates a message that goes viral: You care and they matter.

## Coaching Moments

All "no" answers need to be addressed.

| Question | Answer (Yes or No) |
|---|---|
| **1.** Have you developed relationships with receptionists, security guards, and others with a broad view into the organization? | |
| **2.** Have you identified, categorized, and developed a plan for engaging those who are resisting change? | |
| **3.** If you have a "Stymie Stan" on your team, have you engaged HR and developed a plan to remove the person and transition to new leadership? | |

# Part III
# People

# 7 Reading Minds and Other Methods for Assessing Progress

**S**o you've navigated the politics and launched your change initiative. Now you've got to keep things moving forward. No matter how successful you were with your launch, this is the point where things can go radically wrong if you're not exceptionally people savvy. Tracking progress seems like it should be black and white: You're moving forward in your schedule or you're not. New processes are producing results or they're not. Customers are more satisfied or they're not. In fact, it's not that easy.

At this stage in the game, you need more than a crackerjack project manager checking boxes. A mind reader would be nice, but since that's impossible, in this chapter I offer some methods for accurately assessing progress—or in other words, getting the straight dope.

During my first year as the director of operations of the transportation division at Georgia-Pacific, we ran into a problem with shipments. The sales department was screaming at us because customers were getting their products late. I checked in with the team. They told me that only 5 percent of shipments were affected. I reported that up to management. Again and again they told me 5 percent, and I reported it up, over a six-week period. Meanwhile, we implemented a system that would tell us exactly what percentage of deliveries was arriving on time.

I'll never forget the day I got the first report. I looked at the screen and saw not 5 percent, but 50 percent. I blinked twice and the number didn't change. Fifty percent! After two hours of staring at my computer, I finally typed up an e-mail to executive management. The subject line? "I WAS WRONG."

The gap between 5 and 50 is where so many initiatives veer off course. Was my team willfully deceiving me, or was their perception off? In that case, I believe it was the latter—they were still getting their arms around what was happening. But both kinds of distortion happen in the process of new initiatives, when anxiety is heightened and a certain amount of chaos looms. People also have a natural impulse to deliver good news right away and withhold bad news until they see if they can fix it.

As a leader, manage the "people" element of reporting carefully, so that you can be sure your data is good. Developing high-trust relationships, discussed later in Part III, is extremely important at the high level. But down on the ground, there are a number of people-oriented practices a leader can use to ensure that he or she is getting good data.

Start with finding the right data: those that reveal meaningful progress. It's kind of like watching a NASCAR race. One car can be in the lead but then lose the race because the team didn't plan its pit stops correctly. Your team could be plowing through their "completed tasks" list, but failing to validate whether the tasks were executed successfully. Suddenly, the project's equivalent of a tire flies off because the team forgot to replace the lug nuts.

Ask your teams to be specific in their reports. Throw out those "stoplight updates" that show progress as green, yellow, or red. They're close to useless. I have seen more initiatives go from green to red faster than a Ferrari. When people try to add nuance, it's only confusing. For example, in one update I received, the item was green-ish yellow. "What in the world does that mean?" I asked. The response was, "It is on track, but could get off if this doesn't get done by a certain time."

Reports should instead itemize the actions that were planned for the period, with checkmarks for *complete* and *incomplete*, and a notes section to describe how those actions were validated. The comments can't be general; they have to be specific. For example, you want infor-mation as detailed as, "ran a set of order and invoice transactions for the month of XX and summary reports for the same time period and the numbers matched penny-for-penny to the transactions and reports from the current system." If you don't get that level of detail, ask the team for it.

We learn by *doing*. We build relationships by doing. We finesse problems by doing. We validate or invalidate assumptions by doing. Therefore, your most important metric is, "What's getting done, and how do we know it was done right?"

## Read Faces, Not Reports

When it comes to accurately assessing progress, presentations do tell you something. A couple of rules of thumb: The prettier the slides, the worse the news. It doesn't take graphics or animations to convey good news, so the more things that are spinning, the more you need to worry. Likewise, the thicker the presentation, the worse the news. Good news is always beautifully simple.

The real secret to finding the truth between 5 percent and 50 percent (to use my previous example) is ignoring the PowerPoint and reading the people. You need to go where they are and meet them face-to-face. In more than 30 years of traveling to places all around the world—England, France, China, India, Russia, South America, Africa,

Israel, Singapore, Thailand, Vietnam, you name it—I found that every culture I touched shared one thing in common: the language of their faces and bodies. A smile is a smile anywhere in the world, as is a laugh. Conversely, a frown is a frown, as is a cry.

People's body language allows you to see what they are feeling, regardless of what is being said or reported. E-mails and texts fail in this regard, and so does video. You can see people's body language on video, but you can't feel it. A room full of people gives off a certain energy that you have to be physically present to absorb.

Here are a few techniques to get the best results from in-person reporting.

- Go to the project site to get the updates. People's behavior changes when they have to come to you, especially if you sit in corporate and on the executive floor. In that environment, people become more formal and self-conscious, and candor suffers.

- Ask all of the core team members to be in the room when the update is given. The fewer people in the room, the harder it is to determine fact from fiction. You have fewer facial expressions to see and less body language to read and energy to feel. The likelihood is greater that there will be people present who haven't rehearsed.

- Before the update, take some time to walk through the team's work area. What you see will help you get a read on how things are going. Do people greet you, or do they lean into their computer screens? (The latter is not a good sign.) Is everyone frowning? Look at the huddles around the water cooler. Do they suddenly break up as you approach, or do they continue their conversation or even invite you to join? These telling signs may seem obvious, but you'll miss them if you fail to arrive early.

- When the person is giving the update, watch not only his body language, but also everyone else's in the room. Are they looking at the floor or the ceiling while the person is talking? (Not good.) Are their expressions blank or incredulous? (Not good.) Note: "He's talking total BS" is an expression that's hard to miss.

- Watch posture: Are people slouched in their chairs? (Not good.)

- At the end of the update, open the floor to discuss people's concerns. If people exchange glances and there is awkward silence, you've got a problem. If you're really lucky, you'll catch a few "Are we going to tell him?" looks. These are signs that you need to dig deeper, but don't bother doing it during the meeting. You might have follow-up meetings with subsets of the group, or jump straight to an anonymous survey.

## Adjust for Culture

When it comes to reading people in person, different cultures have different telling signs. For example, within organizations that have a top-down, command and control culture, people are very reserved in their communication. Everyone pays careful attention to protocol and looks up the chain for cues on how to act. This is typical in highly regulated industries that emphasize standard procedures to avoid disasters such as personal injuries or business disruptions. Dealing with this kind of culture, body language becomes even more important because people are more hesitant to speak up or to speak in opposition to their leaders.

Conversely, people within highly collaborative organizations are expressive, not only in their body language but also in their conversation. Typically these are organizations that compete on creativity and innovation. At Medtronic, for example, people never hesitated to tell me what they thought, particularly if they felt we were moving away from the company's mission. Here you can be more confident that people will speak up, but you still have to evaluate their accuracy. Watch how the leader of a group reacts as his or her people are speaking. If leader seems to be uncomfortable, interrupts them, or jumps in afterward to put a spin on what they said, those are warning signs.

Both cultures, of course, have boundaries and, therefore, politics and personal agendas. In other words, there is no perfectly transparent culture. Mavericks, the captains of "telling it like it is," have a difficult time in both. In a command and control culture, they're constantly questioning standard operating procedures and other parameters set by leaders. Collaborative cultures, meanwhile, deal with contrasting ideas with compromise, which is not a concept that passionate mavericks are comfortable with.

## Never Kill the Messenger

If you want good data, make it safe for people to admit mistakes and challenges. How hard you have to work at that will depend on the culture and leader that precede you. I was in a talent review meeting once and a person's name came up. Someone mentioned that the person had messed up in the past. When I asked what the person had done, the response was, "He was the lead on a study and management didn't agree with his recommendations. They thought the analysis was faulty and also incomplete." (Thinking back to my freight-rating experience, I wondered who was really at fault, the employee or his managers.) I then asked when the problem had happened. The person had to think about it, and then came up with "five or six years ago."

I shook my head, incredulous. "Well, I used to wear diapers but I hope my mother isn't still holding it against me!"

Everyone laughed, but I knew then that I was dealing with a culture problem. They saw mistakes only as demerits, not as opportunities to learn and grow. I knew I'd have to teach people a new way of operating, and in the meantime, account for low transparency with the same methods I've described in this chapter.

There are three ways to encourage people to be open about challenges, issues, and outright failures. First, make your position explicit: Let people know that change means challenges, and the only time those challenges are a problem is when they're not brought to light so that the team can address them. Transparency is of higher value to you as a leader than perfection.

Second, set the example. Own up to your own errors in real time, but also tell stories of past failures—times when *you were wrong.*

Finally, when people do come to you with problems, respond in a way that makes them and others feel safe to own up to future errors. Keep your cool and resist the blame game. The goal is to find solutions, not punish offenders. Once the problem is rectified, you can better evaluate how the individuals involved contributed both to the problem *and* the solution.

## Combating Groupthink with Anonymous Feedback

There are times when people fail to speak up because "everyone else" seems happy with progress and confident in the project, so they dismiss their concerns instead of coming forward, often with disastrous results. The more the change leader and his core team sit in conference rooms, the more groupthink sets in. People stop being objective and analytical and instead find ways to confirm their points of view. To use a colloquialism, people start "smoking their own dope."

I experienced this while implementing a new manufacturing system at one of Medtronic's biggest facilities. The system was going to fundamentally change how data flowed through the organization. The project leader was solid, and things had been moving forward on schedule. Throughout the project, there were update meetings in which the business, manufacturing, and technical teams reported that everything was right on target. At our final meeting, we had a unanimous thumbs-up to go live. Go, team.

Twenty-four hours later, all hell had broken loose. The reports were wrong and operators were having difficulty using the system. As a result, sales, distribution, and manufacturing were not on the same page. Products weren't being made, inventory wasn't being fulfilled, and worst yet, orders weren't being shipped. This was the worst possible outcome because customers were directly affected.

Executive leaders were quick to ask the question on everyone's mind, most of all mine: Why the $%* didn't we know we weren't ready to go live? As we dug ourselves out of the situation, what had happened became clear: The list of tasks had been completed, yes sir, including training the front-line users of the new system. But trained or not, they weren't comfortable using it, and no one had wanted to be the one to speak up about it. Within management, there were also reservations, but the site had a very strong and respected leader. If he said things were going well, his people nodded and swallowed their concerns. (It's amazing how one strong personality can influence the thinking of a group as a whole.) In addition, the IT system introduced many new processes. When they tested them, they never compared the results against the ones produced by the old processes. If they had, they would have seen they were different and they would have immediately known there was a problem.

I take responsibility. I broke my number one rule by trusting PowerPoints and stoplight reports. Shame on me. I also didn't do the two things that would have tipped us off to the trouble spots that lay beneath all those cheery reports. One, taking a temperature check in person, the value of which I already discussed. And two, I should have conducted an anonymous survey of everyone touching the project. Anonymity in situations where groupthink has taken hold is particularly helpful. The question you may ask is, "How will I know that groupthink has set in?" Chances are, if you're leading any kind of change other than incremental, and at every single meeting all you're getting is nods and smiles, something is up.

The value of a survey is not just that it frees people to speak their truth without consequences, it's also that it spurs them to think critically by asking for their unique opinions. They are forced to take a moment to pause and reflect. Any hesitations they've been suppressing tend to surface pretty quickly when they actually stop to think independently. Make sure people understand that the survey is completely anonymous and only you, your HR person, and your communications person will be reviewing the results. You don't want anyone's boss to pressure them to rate the initiative highly.

The survey doesn't need to be complicated. In fact, you need to keep it extremely short so that people will actually complete it. Just ask two simple questions:

1. On a scale of 1 to 5, with 5 being the best, how likely is it that the initiative will be a success?

2. If you didn't rate it a 5, what needs to be done to make it a 5?

Survey everyone on the project at least every other month and before the "go live" decision is made.

Surveys work well for smaller projects in which it's easy to wrap your arms around the issues and potential flash points. For larger projects, bring in the big guns: The third-party audit.

## Third-Party Evaluations

For major transformations, third-party evaluations are your friends. An objective, in-depth evaluation can help you cut through politics and personal agendas to determine your true state of readiness. They can also be very helpful if you run into any postimplementation problems, since their dispassionate point of view can help everybody see the issues in the context: You've made exhaustive changes and that causes exhausting problems. Within the team, people often get so focused on the problems that they don't see the broader success of the initiative. As one of my former bosses used to say, "It may be that only 5 percent of the people were affected, but that's 100 percent if you're one of them." He's absolutely right, but the fact is that change initiatives, even those led and executed responsibly, involve a certain amount of experimentation (i.e., error). A third-party audit can help you make that case, especially in those moments in which everyone who campaigned against the change in the first place is now campaigning to have it reversed.

That kind of opposition tends to strike exactly when all of your focus and all of your people's focus is on fixing the issues and getting things working—which will, after all, be the best proof that you were right. Bring in that third party, as I did after another huge implementation went live and had start-up issues. The third party assessed the situation and told us that our issues were nothing compared to what other companies making the same change had experienced. When the executive team heard that, they finally stood down. We got to work and, in a few weeks, everything was running smoothly. With continued interference, a few weeks could have been a few months, which could have led to lost accounts or a rollback to the old, inferior way of doing things.

Even with a third-party audit, your adversaries may try to dismiss the third party as biased. It's a fair complaint if you're the one deciding whether they did a "good" job and signing their checks. Avoid that pitfall by having the consultants report to an organization besides yours. For example, have them report to your internal audit or accounting department.

## Don't Forget Your Hubs

When it comes to completing your collection of objective, independent feedback, no source is more powerful and valuable than a hub.

If you remember, I recommended against putting hubs on your core team to protect their influence. Here we see another reason why: It shields them from groupthink. They're always on the outside looking in. That maintains the independence of their points of view. It also makes them natural havens for people—those on the core team or within the broader organization—who have concerns that they're afraid to voice to official leaders or even immediate colleagues. A hub's neutral ears will hear it all and report anything out to you that might lead to trouble. (As a rule, hubs are not gossips or spies. They have the success of the project and the company as a whole in mind.)

A hub's informed assessment of your progress can save you from operational problems and political ones, too. I once stepped in to a hornet's nest and was rescued by a hub. While working in the transportation division at GP, we were finding that having to go to corporate IT every time we needed reporting was a real problem; we needed data and insight more quickly and frequently than they could accommodate. To solve the problem, I acquired a computer that would allow us to produce reports ourselves. The corporate IT group went crazy. They thought I was trying to build my own "shadow IT" group outside of their control. If that's what I was doing, I was in trouble because the computer on which I was building my new empire was old enough that it had been phased out of service by another division within the company.

Two of the top IT guys scheduled a meeting with my boss, framed as a "friendly update lunch." Their real agenda was to shut me down. They probably would have been successful if a hub hadn't gotten wind of it. He let my boss know that he should include me in the meeting and why.

You should have seen their faces when I got off the elevator to go to lunch with the group. They went white as ghosts. At the restaurant, small talk prevailed until the last 10 minutes. At that point, they informed my boss that the computer I had been given would cost the company tens of thousands of dollars—an "irresponsible expense" when it was their group who should be handling the reporting anyway. They didn't just want to shut down my reporting initiative; they wanted to discredit my leadership in general.

Well, I was prepared. I whipped out an e-mail from the division that had given me the computer. It confirmed that its value on the books was "$0.00" because they had depreciated it fully. Everyone's chins dropped, and for a precious few seconds, I felt like Peter Falk on *Colombo,* the guy with every answer. I only needed a cigar.

The primary instigator just shook his head. As he got the check, all he could say was, "James, you got me on this one."

My boss was impressed, and on the way back from lunch he asked me to develop a division-wide IT strategy. And that's where the true empire building began, all thanks to a hub.

## *Chapter 7 in Tweets*

- Never be afraid to write an e-mail with the subject line "I WAS WRONG."

- Trust people, not PowerPoints.

- Stoplight reports alone are useless. Track action—specific tasks completed and validated.

- Get status updates face-to-face with as many people present as possible, then watch people's body language.

- When someone makes a mistake, take care: A leader's response defines transparency levels going forward.

- Top tools to overcome groupthink and protect an initiative from political attack: surveys and third-party audits.
- Leverage the perspective of hubs, the best source of straight talk in an organization.

## Coaching Moments

All "no" answers need to be addressed.

| Question | Answer (Yes or No) |
| --- | --- |
| **1.** Are you having status meetings with all of the core members present and checking progress against the completion of specific actions, rather than relying on "stoplight" reports? | |
| **2.** In the past 60 days, have you conducted an anonymous survey of the core team to gauge members' opinions on how successful the initiative will be? | |
| **3.** If you are close to going live with a technology change, have you had an independent third party assess your readiness? | |
| **4.** Within the past 30 days, have you gotten an internal hub's assessment of the project's progress? | |
| **5.** Do you have a backup plan and have you tested it? | |

# 8 Alignment and Group Dynamics

I shared earlier that people hate the word *standardize*. The truth is that people like standards just fine—as long as they're theirs. Yet at some point in most change initiatives, some degree of standardization is necessary. It's how you achieve the new normal. Getting there requires alignment—not only as the initiative launches, but also as you plow through the sometimes messy business of implementation. Otherwise, your initiative can end up like the United States' conversion to the metric system: You support multiple solutions, with the confusion and inefficiency that inevitably result.

In Part II, Politics, I covered communication strategies for alignment at the launch of initiatives. Now I'm going to focus on tactical strategies for managing group dynamics. This is how you align and realign, and align and realign, your people over the course of an initiative.

I call my general approach to this the "Six-Pack Approach." I came up with the phrase one day when someone took a shot at me in a meeting by asking, "James, what is it that you do?" I was a senior vice president at the time, and apparently doing too good a job of leading from behind. I was making it look easy! (It isn't.) Fortunately, I was thinking on my toes that day.

"I'm like that little plastic thing that holds a six-pack together," I said. "People don't think it's worth much until they try to carry six cans without it."

## The Six-Pack Approach

An organization is not a Super Big Gulp, it's a six-pack. And alignment isn't opening up all the cans—the many various business units, functional divisions, and even individual employees—and dumping them into one container, it's getting them lined up and moving in the same direction.

My approach has three steps, all of which are repeated as needed over the course of an initiative as differences arise, politics flare, and challenges are met.

### Find Common Ground

I'm a firm believer that no matter how different the players are, they always share some kind of common ground. As I've said before, common ground, not compromise, is your friend. But the way to find it isn't to bring everyone together right at the outset. When change is making people feel insecure, they act first and foremost to protect their own boundaries. Bring them together in a group, and they'll focus on their differences and adopt a "my turf, your turf" attitude.

The business units at Medtronic provide a great example. Another hurdle we jumped during my time was related to regulatory oversight, which had evolved such that problems in one business unit could lead to greater scrutiny of all the others. As a result, for the first time, we needed to create and enforce best practices for quality management across all the units. I've mentioned before that each business unit regarded itself as its own "state." Each thought *it* followed the best practice and argued that standardization was impossible because they weren't making the same products.

Our first meeting was a complete waste of time. People from each unit spent the entire meeting explaining to me how they were different—which was obvious before they ever started talking. But the fact was, regulatory assessment of quality management was identical across all products, so it was clear that standard best practices were possible, too.

The approach I took next is the one I recommend to all of you. I met with each BU head individually and asked them to review their quality standards with me. What I quickly discovered was that they all shared a need for a new IT system to support quality management. Infrastructure is often a source of common ground. In this case it was software, but physical infrastructure or new personnel and roles are often like needs that have gone unfunded.

When I brought the VPs together to talk about IT, alignment around that issue came quickly. Everyone settled on a common system, which got the ball rolling toward a conversation about metrics, bringing us a step closer to our ultimate goal.

When looking for alignment, meet with each stakeholder individually to find the common ground that provides the opportunity for movement.

## Bring People Together to Develop Common Metrics

Metrics provide a unique opportunity. They are the start of a common language in that they require people to agree on the words, and the exact meaning of the words, to describe the metrics. Once a common language develops, boundaries naturally shift and expand, and the idea of a common culture (and shared standards) begins to sound believable.

Metrics are needed for all change initiatives regardless of the function or business. For example, in operations, metrics might be on-time delivery, first-time quality, lead time, and so on. In customer care, you might see metrics to measure customer satisfaction, "no touch" orders, and the performance of our representatives. Whatever the business or function, use metrics that can be benchmarked against other companies.

Common metrics represent a giant leap, so it's no surprise that here, too, standardization is a struggle. Everyone wants their own metrics to become the common ones. Still, you give them a chance to try to figure it out on their own. Set a target date for their delivery of the new metrics and be willing to offer one extension.

In most cases, even after the extension, they'll be log jammed. Now you step up the heat. Bring them together for a two-day workshop, and let them know they can't leave until they finalize metrics. Add heat by scheduling it on a Thursday; no one will want to have to convene on Saturday if they haven't met their objective.

If this approach seems Draconian, that's not by accident. What I've found is that they stop complaining about each other and start complaining about me. Finally they're thinking like a team, and with the looming deadline, they start to apply that mentality to the work at hand.

My involvement is limited. I kick things off the first morning. If facilitation is needed, I hire someone. The only limitation I put on the outcomes is a cap on the number of metrics. Then I check in at the day's close, reminding them that they'll be there every day until they are successful. I come back at noon on the second day and take questions. Finally, I come back around 3:00 P.M. for a walkthrough of the new metrics. I've never arrived and been met with failure.

## Create a Sense of Urgency

While core metrics represent a huge step, the speed at which the organizations adapt to them can be glacial if you don't apply pressure.

All change initiatives need boosts along the way. Enthusiasm waxes and wanes, and opponents to the change act up to slow or stop progress.

The pressure you need arrives in the form of business challenges from customers, investors, competitors, regulators, or internal operators. Clear-cut threats to the health of the organization give new energy to the change initiative if you can make a compelling case for how the two are linked. In the case of quality management best practices at Medtronic, the connection was obvious: Regulators issued enforcement actions at multiple locations. If this happened at the corporate level, the company's ability to do business would be severely restricted for at least two years.

If you need to drum up urgency on a schedule, have a third party do a benchmarking study. Without exception, the study will find areas where your company is lagging. Do make sure that the leaders in the affected areas get a chance to review the report before the COO or CEO, otherwise they'll see it as an attack and work the politics of damage control. Any boundaries you had succeeded in lifting will smack back down.

When creating a sense of urgency, the change leader has to maintain balance. You don't want to come across as an alarmist or as someone who sensationalizes events to fit your agenda. Let your hubs start the conversation, so that the leaders in question come to you to ask about the situation. There's your opening.

What's important is that you're ready for this moment with a plan of action that operationalizes the progress toward alignment you've made so far. Otherwise the rock you've been pushing uphill could, as people react to a threat, get pushed backward and run you over.

With people's energy renewed, leadership motivated, and a clear plan at the ready, alignment finally gets operationalized and turns into action.

## Alignment Sessions

Previously I mentioned putting people together in a room so that they can hash out and commit to a shared solution. There are a few things I always make "right" to ensure that they have a successful session. These tips apply to any kind of group decision-making or problem-solving process.

First, pick the right room. It should be big and open enough that people can get up and walk around. If the space is claustrophobic, people close their minds. An open room helps open minds to new ideas. I can't provide any scientific proof for that, but I've seen it play out many times.

Second, place the leader (whether it's you or someone else) in the right position. That's the middle of the room, where he or she can see everyone and hear what their mouths and their bodies are saying. But note that the leader should not facilitate the session. Generally speaking, the leader shouldn't contribute much more than opening comments. You can't facilitate, listen, watch, and learn all at the same time. Delegate responsibility to a dedicated facilitator to probe and push during the meetings. Otherwise, people will think that you have taken a position and it will bias the meeting.

Third, set the right mood. In your opening comments, put every-one in the right mind-set. They are no longer representatives of their individual functions in the company. They are one team, a board of directors being asked to make a strategic decision that best serves the company's interests. Each person needs to bring an informed point of view and an open mind to the work at hand. The leader's role is only to add facts to the discussion as needed and to make a final decision if the team is unable to reach alignment.

Fourth, keep the people right. Remind everyone that being on the same team doesn't mean they won't have disagreements. Debating different points of view is part of the process. People should check their egos and be respectful. All discussion should be open to the entire group; no side meetings.

## When and How to Make an Executive Decision

As a leader, you want to hand off decision making to others as much as you can. Giving people control over the details goes a long way to ease resistance to the overall plans for change. Again, the leader's job is to keep the six-pack together, not to micromanage their decision making.

However, there are times when dysfunction takes over and an executive decision is needed to keep things moving. For example, if people still haven't reached alignment after a meeting like the one outlined previously, step in. The challenge is finding a way to handle it that doesn't leave people feeling like you're ruling by fiat.

I had to make an executive decision once when our tech team at Medtronic was deadlocked in deciding between two different technologies from two different companies. Initially, I turned the decision making over to them, but when several sessions over two months failed to result in a decision, I had to get involved. They had become two warring camps who were wasting meeting after meeting talking at each other without really listening. Worse, discussions were devolving into personal attacks. The group was beyond the point where I could lock them in a room and trust that they could reach a resolution.

I could have just met with the suppliers and made an independent decision. That would have gotten us moving forward, but it would have completely eroded the trust I had been trying to build and it would have made everyone involved feel powerless.

Instead, I called everyone together. I explained carefully why I was getting involved. I let them know I'd listen to all their arguments and make the best decision I could, but at that point, moving forward was more important than the subtleties that were miring them in gridlock.

Over the course of two meetings, I let the two factions make their cases and then I made a decision.

Any time that you have to take agency away from the team, take the time to explain why—and make sure you have a good reason. Once you've made a decision, take care in how you announce it. Start by summarizing the various arguments so it is clear that you heard and understood them. Then, be clear and transparent about how you made your choice. Most people will support a decision that is different from theirs if they feel that their points of view were given serious consideration.

In dealing with our tech team, I also made sure that the team knew that in the future, they needed to find a way to come to resolution together. If we ever got into a situation again where people felt so strongly about a supplier that they were looking sideways at their own teammates, they should go work for that company, not Medtronic.

To bring perspective to the situation, I often close this kind of discussion by sharing my own approach to the times I've had to decide whether to support a decision I didn't agree with. I have three criteria:

1. Is the decision an ethical one?

2. Does the decision have the potential to create a disaster that the organization can't recover from?

3. Is the leader the type of person who will make adjustments if the decision creates problems down the line?

If the answer to those three questions is yes, I support the leader and the decision 100 percent.

## Brokering Deals

Sometimes making an executive decision isn't appropriate or within your power. In such cases, you have to find a way to broker a deal. I've often found that I'm more successful when I approach a negotiation with the understanding that, at the end of the day, what we're brokering is trust. What do I need to do so that they trust that I will do my best to meet their needs within the change I am advocating for?

For example, when we consolidated distribution centers at Medtronic, one of the business unit operations VPs was concerned because he would no longer control the centers, yet he would still be the one to get the calls from his bosses if shipments were missed. In such a situation, he'd have to say, "Let me check with James," which isn't what you want to have to tell your boss. I've been in that position before, and I can tell you it is not a good position to be in.

Mind you, he didn't tell any of this to me. He was just doing whatever was in his power to resist the change. To broker trust, I talked to my hubs and sponsors. They understood the politics of the organization well enough to know the currency at play. A hub explained to me the source of the VP's resistance, and together we came up with a way to broker trust. We'd put someone in the VP's group in charge of the shared service that we were creating. That was enough to give him the control that he needed.

Another tactic I like to use when brokering deals is finding a way to test both solutions: the one I'm offering and the one proposed by the dissenting party. We then let results determine which approach is better. This creates trust immediately, especially when I let the other party establish the success criteria and metrics for our experiment. For example, I once let a business unit use a different third party to outsource its warehouse operations than what we chose for the rest of the company. We needed to cut costs while waiting to develop the long-term plan of consolidating all the warehouses. In the end, it was the right move—it turned out that their choice suited our requirements much better. It was one of the many times that giving people latitude to make their own decisions while working toward alignment has paid off.

## The Importance of Reaching Up

Every change initiative faces challengers and challenges. The moment you think you have alignment, the wind shifts and someone has a new concern that seems to throw all your hard work into jeopardy.

Don't make the mistake of trying to handle it all alone. You are not all-knowing—far from it. From the beginning to the end of your work, constantly reach up for advice and direction from senior-level mentors and sponsors. The dynamics influencing behavior at the top of the organization are not always visible to you. Furthermore, these people acquired a lot of wisdom on their way up. Put it into service.

The difference between a mentor and a sponsor is that the former opens your mind by sharing advice, ideas, and suggestions. The latter opens other's minds; they advocate for you, opening doors on your behalf. You need both. I go to my mentors before I start a change initiative and along the way for fresh ideas and a broader perspective than I can bring to the table. I go to my sponsors for background on the key players' bosses and what their perspectives and agendas might be.

Early in my career, I avoided reaching up for help, usually until it was too late. I was making the mistake of thinking that I needed to impress my mentors and sponsors by always looking like I had all the answers and was in total control. That was how I showed them my importance. In fact, the more important you are in an organization, the more advice you need, because the stakes are greater and the politics are more complex. Admitting you don't have all the answers is a sign of maturity and good sense—the proof that you deserve the responsibility you've been given.

*Chapter 8 in Tweets*

- Six-pack leadership: A leader is the plastic piece that you barely notice—until you try to carry six cans without it.

- Teams accept executive decisions when they know they've been heard. Take the time to show them.

- Common metrics in an organization are the start of a common language.

- In negotiations, what's really on the table is trust. Broker trust and you'll find resolution.

- Change agents need VIP help. Don't forget to reach up for advice and support.

## Coaching Moments

All "no" answers need to be addressed.

| Question | Answer (Yes or No) |
|---|---|
| **1.** Have you developed common, clearly defined metrics for success that everyone is in agreement with? | |
| **2.** Did you get advice from the core team and key stakeholders before you made your last decision, and did they feel like you listened to them? (Have your HR person ask them this question, because they will be more candid with him or her than with you.) | |

| Question | Answer (Yes or No) |
|---|---|
| **3.** Did you get advice from your sponsors and mentors prior to the last major decision you made? | |
| **4.** Would the last person you brokered a deal with say that he or she trusts you? (Have HR ask the person this question. If the response is "no," follow up personally.) | |

# 9 Master the Humble Art of Building Trust

**W**ithout trust, there is no leadership. Trust translates directly into loyalty, candor, and high performance among your employees and colleagues. Aside from all that, when everything else goes wrong, it's relationships that save your bacon.

It was my relationship skills that saved me during that freight-rating debacle that I've come back to several times now. After botching the politics while delivering the "worst idea ever," I ended up with a promotion. Later, I found out why the senior executive who called me out had a complete change of heart. A hub who I had gotten close to within the transportation division had been quietly and effectively advocating to him on my behalf. The hub convinced the executive that my suggestion was solid, and he vouched for my character and future potential, too. The hub would never have stepped up the way that he did, or have been able to speak to who I was, without the strong relationship that I had built with him. Above all, he trusted that I would do right by the organization and the people I became responsible for.

The fact is, when you get the politics or the priorities wrong, the "people" part of the triad can often save you—if you've gone out of your way to give them reasons to do so. (Note: If you get *both* the priorities and the politics wrong, you're probably sunk. So don't do that.)

Trust is often more important than any practical skill you might offer. When my boss in the transportation division at GP asked me to design an overall IT strategy, as I related earlier, he knew that I didn't have the experience. But strategy he could teach me. Integrity was what I brought to the table. He knew it from our interactions and from the reports he got from his hubs. He could trust that I'd have his back.

Senior executives surround themselves with people they trust. To join that inner circle, change leaders need to be willing and able to build high-trust relationships—and not just with management. Trust is important up and down the line. Trust is how you get to know what truly matters to people, to cut through politics and successfully campaign for change. Trust ensures that people will follow you even in the most difficult moments, when they might have otherwise chosen a different path. It even ensures that people will follow you when you discover you chose the wrong path. (That day will come, because no one is always right.)

When people trust their leader, their senses of security and significance endure even when everything around them is changing. Trust makes it possible to stay the course.

But how do you build trust, particularly when your teams are so big that you can't sit down one-on-one with everyone? That's the focus of this chapter.

## Building Inner-Circle Relationships

Before turning to your teams, I'd like to spend a minute on those closest to you. The most effective leaders build airtight relationships with their bosses, their peers, their hubs, and their sponsors (and not all these relationships are mutually exclusive, of course). Your energy will be well invested.

Every change agent needs a great relationship with his or her boss. It almost goes without saying, but that's how you get the latitude and the benefit of the doubt to run with ambitious, exploratory ideas. Many books on business relationships will tell you to try to build up the personal side of your relationship with dinner or golf. There's nothing wrong with that, but I believe that the best way to win trust and respect from the person you work for is to understand his or her strategic, operational, and tactical priorities and help advance them. Focus on the tactical and operational priorities in particular, because they are more likely to be achievable within a year's time. Just by working together toward a goal, you'll build trust. When you achieve it, your relationship will be cemented. Maybe *then* it's time to ask him or her to dinner, to celebrate.

Sucking up never works with anyone who's worth sucking up to, so don't bother. Trust is built through action and commitment. Always give your honest opinion, but once a decision is made, support it, assuming it's ethical and legal. Telling others "I'm just following orders" does not constitute support. Never throw your boss under the bus, and make sure he or she is your first stop with any news affecting the business—bad or good.

Building trust with professional peers isn't any different. Know their priorities and do everything you can to support them. One cardinal rule that I had with my fellow senior vice presidents was that we'd never disagree in public, especially in front of the board. I realized how important this was during one particular board meeting. One of the senior vice presidents was asked about the budget he was given by the CFO. His response was extremely negative, and he griped that he was having to shut down critical projects to achieve it. (The fact that the CEO, who had signed off on the budget, was in the bathroom at that moment the question was asked probably fueled his sudden attack of candor.) What bothered everybody was that he had been personally involved in the budget process and knew that the company's financial challenges that year required some difficult decisions. He shared in the decision-making process and now was blaming our choices on the CFO. His griping didn't get him anywhere, and worse, made it look like he was more concerned about himself than about the health of the overall organization.

As for hubs, sincerity and respect go a long way. That said, the best way to get tight with a hub is to empower him or her with your budget and backing. I remember meeting with a hub within our corporate technology and science group at Medtronic. He told me about two initiatives, both outside of his group, that needed funding. Because both ideas had merit, I immediately agreed to fund a POC for one using $25,000 of my budget and to be the executive champion of the other, which was enterprise-wide.

As for sponsors, I again depart from the conventional wisdom, which tells you to actively court these important relationships. My experience has been that the most influential sponsors don't want or need to be courted. They are looking for quality people to groom for leadership. They choose *you*. The way to attract them is by showing leadership wherever you are in your career. You do need to make sure that you're visible in your organization, but do so by being extraordinary: speaking up in meetings; sharing good ideas; taking on work; carving out new responsibilities for yourself; being proactive; and, when needed, speaking truth to power. That's the way to get on the radar of a sponsor.

My most important sponsors have emerged from the woodwork exactly when I needed them. At one point, when I was a group director at GP, I was having tremendous difficulty getting a business unit leader to see that his IT costs were twice what they should have been. Sure, he didn't have an IT background, but he was convinced (probably by the guy he was buying them from) that their IT systems were giving them competitive advantage. He wrote a blistering e-mail summarizing his point of view: I didn't know what the hell I was talking about.

He copied everyone on it, including the executive vice president that his business unit reported to and the companywide HR leader.

It was a very low moment for me. Even though I knew I was right, being denounced in front of a big chunk of the company felt like a major defeat. I was down in the dumps as I was driving home, and then I got a phone call from the executive vice president, who had received the e-mail. He told me not to worry; he knew I was in the right and I had his full support. He told me to keep on pressing the issue. Without that call, I might have given up on the issue, which would have been bad for the organization, and ultimately bad for my career. That sponsor didn't disappear after that; three years later I was on his team.

## Step Outside of Your Own Boundaries

As your responsibility grows and you rise in your career as a change leader, you'll find yourself constantly asking the people who work for you to step outside their boundaries. That's what change requires. They'll be more likely to trust and follow if they've seen that you, too, are willing to leave your comfort zone and put emotional skin in the game. Doing so allows you to transcend differences and find common ground, the space where trust begins.

When I became the vice president of the GP Distribution Division's mid-Atlanta region, people thought I'd never be able to build trust with the most important constituency for success: the customer. This was completely new to me, since this was my first role out of the safe warren of IT. I was also a city slicker who until then had only worked in the trucking part of the company. Now I would be dealing with the lumber part of the business, working with customers who ran rural lumberyards and looked at anyone in a suit with one eyebrow cocked. The business had been struggling, and about $700 million in annual revenues were on the line if I couldn't find a way to turn it around. I wouldn't just need to build trust with customers, but also with the sales people, many of whom were suspicious that my arrival was a misguided corporate blunder.

To grow revenue, one of our salespeople, Dan, came up with a great incentive plan. Our customers were huge NASCAR fans, so we would offer free race tickets to anyone who increased his or her year-over-year purchases by 10 percent or more. The promotion was a big hit, and when the first race approached, I surprised everyone by announcing I'd attend along with Dan.

A buzz went through my organization, but it was my mother who first said to my face what everyone was chattering about: "Don't too many black people go to those races," she said, incredulous when I told her. I then let on that the race was in Richmond, Virginia. "I'll be prayin' for you," she added. In the weeks before the race, she wasn't the only one, white or black, to say something similar.

The track at Richmond was enormous, boasting 90,000 seats, all of which were full the day of our race. From where we entered, we had to walk halfway around the perimeter to get to our seats. After we passed about 30,000 people, Dan turned to me and said, "James, I think that you may be the only African American here." I smiled. "That's true, but consider this. Anyone who looks twice at me isn't thinking, 'What's he doing here?' they're thinking, 'Who the hell brought him?'"

The look on Dan's face was priceless. We both broke out into grins. When we got to our seats, our customers were already there. There were about 15 of them, and I sat next to our biggest customer in that region. He was about 65 years old, the owner of the company, and he had his son with him. He had been a racing enthusiast since he was a boy. When I told him that this was my first race, he became my passionate tutor. He told me everything to look for and then had me put on earphones that let me listen to the drivers communicating with their teams.

Watching and listening during the pit stops, I was in awe; I had never before seen real-time precision teamwork on that level. After the race, the group asked me what I thought about it, watching carefully as I responded. It was easy for me to be genuinely enthusiastic, especially when I started talking about the teamwork. They all nodded their heads, smiling, and continued the conversation. We were all leading companies, even if they were different sizes. Appreciation for quality teamwork was common ground. If it was a test, I had passed with flying colors. The event was a huge success, and I left knowing that I had cemented some important relationships.

Word of the day's events spread rapidly throughout the division. The question of whether I could relate to customers had been answered, and the sales force looked at me with new eyes. Within three months, a second region was added to my responsibilities.

I knew from the start that I could be a good leader for the organization. Once I demonstrated that I was willing and able to step into their world with both feet, everyone else knew it, too.

## Eight Practices for Building Trust

You don't have to go as far as NASCAR to step outside of your boundaries. You can do it within your company's walls. You could spend an afternoon having a call center employee train you to work the phones. You could take time during a group meeting to share a time you made a mistake. You could organize an evening event, or simply join employees for lunch. These are all opportunities to let people see beyond your job title.

Remember Ernie, my boss at Pepperidge Farm? I told you earlier that he won our trust by letting us know how valuable our work was, and serving us steak dinners to prove it. He was the top boss, yet he did even the janitors' onboarding personally. That meant something to me. I believed him when he said doing our jobs to the letter was

important—so much so that when a fellow janitor failed
the bins on his shift and I didn't have time to clean them
I let Ernie know. Keeping standards high was more important to me
than taking heat for ratting out a peer. Without Ernie's leadership,
I probably would have let it slip. Point being, trust is more than a
"warm fuzzy"—it has real influence on how people behave.

What follows is a list of the eight practices I repeat again and again
to keep the boundaries between me and my teams as fluid as possible.
Over time and with sincere attention, they lead to high levels of trust
and mutual respect.

### 1. Ask a hub to introduce you.

This creates a halo effect, predisposing people to give you the
benefit of the doubt. Of course, in order for this to work, you've
got to gain the hub's trust first—otherwise he or she will be reading from your bio, which gets you nowhere. Build that relationship first, so that when the hub is introducing you, he or she is
also vouching for you with a statement like, "I'm getting to know
James personally, but what I've seen so far tells me that he learns,
engages, and does the right thing."

### 2. Break bread on their turf.

I've touched on this several times already. Initial meetings
with the people who will be your partners—leaders, hubs,
mavericks, and so on—should always take place over meals.
Have them pick the restaurant. If you're in a region that's new
to you, you can even have them order. Often you'll find there's
a story or significance to the dish that they choose. Note: Unless
you're allergic, eat as much as you can. Being tepid about their
favorite food isn't the best way to start!

I will always remember a meal I had when I was meeting
with our team in China. We were at a manufacturing location
far away from any major city. There were at least five local people
from the site at the table. I told them that I would eat whatever

they did. In the local custom, the food was placed on a lazy Susan turntable. There was some type of chicken in a very big pot that they had ordered. When it came around for my second helping, the chicken's feet popped out of the pot. All eyes turned on me to see how I would react. In my mind, I said, "Damn! Those are chicken feet!" However, I immediately put them on my plate and asked casually, "Do I use my chopsticks to eat them?" Everyone just smiled and looked at each other in approval.

### 3. Speak their language.

This goes for traveling to foreign offices, but also for the unique cultures within your company. Certain words carry significance. For example, at Medtronic, invoking our mission of "improving lives" got people's attention. At Georgia Pacific, any words related to safety had weight. Listen to people and you'll learn their buzzwords quickly—or ask a hub to bring you up to speed.

### 4. Acknowledge people, especially front-line employees.

It means a lot to people when senior-level leaders greet and meet them. In doing so, you're offering two of the three things people value most: security and significance. That means that when you lead them through change, those things are protected. Believe it or not, a simple "hello" with a smile can make people feel that you value them.

Leaders sometimes don't realize that their acknowledgment makes a real impact. People don't just notice how they are greeted, but also how the leaders are greeting others. If you only smile and glad hand with certain people when you come into a room, they see that. If they aren't among them, their senses of significance take a hit.

Always acknowledging people is easier said than done. *Always* means always, not just when you have time. When walking the halls, you can't get so caught up in your thinking that you ignore people as they walk by. Nothing gets in the way of building trust more than being hot then cold in your behavior. I remember one IT director during my programming days who walked by me every single morning without saying hello. When he finally stuck his head into my office one day and said, "Hello, my name is XXX, what's yours?" it scared the living hell out of me. Far from building trust, his appearance made me think, "What was *that* about?" I wasn't surprised when a couple of weeks later his "resignation" was announced. It was too little too late.

**5. Engage people.**

Schedule time dedicated to asking people what they feel and think. Hold structured sessions and listen, listen, listen. The most important aspect of getting this right comes after the sessions end. You have to follow up and let them know what you are doing with their suggestions. Even if the answer is "nothing," they need to understand why. Otherwise you're just patronizing them, which destroys trust.

**6. Share your weaknesses.**

This can be surprisingly difficult; leadership can create self-consciousness. After all, people are watching your every move. But what I've learned is that failing to acknowledge my weaknesses—for example, times I've made mistakes—diminishes their trust. We're all human, and if people don't see the signs of that, they just assume you're hiding them, which is the opposite of trust. Instead, open up to them. You'll find that they respond in kind.

**7. Create safety to discuss mistakes.**

The fact that I acknowledge my own mistakes goes a long way toward teaching people that mistakes are a normal part of the business of change. But when I am in charge of a new group, I always make sure to let them know what will happen if they come to me with a mistake. I won't chew them out or hang them out to dry. (Do that, and there won't be a next time.) Instead, I'll ask how they're going to fix it and what I can do to help. I never fault someone for a mistake, only for the failure to then learn from it.

I once ignored the recommendation of an e-commerce expert, Gabe, when I tried to implement a data-gathering technology that he flat out told me wouldn't work. He was right, but he never said, "I told you so" or used my mistake against me. Instead, he helped me fix it, and in doing so he created a lifetime ally in me. That's the power of mercy.

**8. Be transparent about the change that's coming.**

You won't make people feel safe by hiding the truth; you'll do it by setting a precedent of sharing as much information as you can. You're not just doing it to build trust, but because you're counting on them to help you figure out a course forward. Make sure you let them know that.

There are four things in particular you should share to ease their anxiety:

(1) The process that will be used to determine exactly what will change, and how.

(2) The people who will be involved in the process. (Make sure that at some point that includes them, even if it's just in the form of a feedback meeting.)

(3) The timing of this process.

(4) When the next update will be.

Again, people fear uncertainty more than anything, so give them things that they can be certain about within the broader environment of change.

## Put Your Pride to the Side

"Pride is the only known disease that makes everyone sick except the person who has it" is a favorite quote of mine. Pride is anathema to leadership. Actually, I would take that a step further to say that more than not being prideful, a leader needs to leave his or her ego at home to be most effective.

As the leader, you don't get to be the hero. Your job is to make heroes out of others, not by "giving" them credit, but by giving them enough responsibility so that when things go right, they actually deserve that credit. Another CEO once told me that his "make or break" question when interviewing senior executives was, "How many people who have worked for you have gone on to higher positions in the organization?" If they can't name several, they're out of the running because it suggests they've failed to nurture their teams, failed to share credit for wins, or in all likelihood, both.

When you shine the spotlight on your team, you win their trust, but the effect goes beyond that. When others in the organization see that you're motivated to help others succeed, not to burnish your own reputation, they start to trust you, too.

Putting your pride to the side means giving others not only credit, but also exposure. When you announce good news, don't hog the stage. Let others involved communicate the win. I know plenty of people who let others speak, but only when it's bad news being shared!

In fact, bad news is when it's your turn to grab the mic. I remember one project in particular that I had been brought in to turn around. Shortly after I came on, the VP of the business unit requested a status update, with the project leader in the room. Before the meeting, I asked the leader to let me do the talking. He must've been afraid I would throw him under the bus, because when we got in the room, he immediately launched into a nervous, rambling explanation of why things had gone wrong. He looked like he was dodging responsibility, as was clear from the concerned faces of the executive team. I kicked the corner of his chair, once, twice, three times, trying to get him to stop—until finally I hit it so hard the chair rocked! That finally did it.

Once I started talking, my approach wasn't to blame him, or anybody. Instead, I led with the fact that I had run into similar problems on some of my own projects in the past. I highlighted the fact that though we were in the ditch, we were course correcting early enough that we wouldn't have to spend too much money getting back on track. We were doing what was needed to assess the situation and develop a plan. I told them we'd come back to them in two weeks with a report on the steps we'd taken.

The VP was happy with the report and even told us he appreciated our candor. The project leader was visibly and audibly relieved. (He actually let out a sigh.) After the meeting, he turned to me and said, "James, how did I do?"

Always honest, I responded, "If I would have had a gun, I would have shot you right between the eyes to get you to stop talking!"

We both laughed, and from then on, he trusted me 100 percent.

In that situation, it was enough not to point a finger. There are other times when I've actually taken the fall for someone else's mistake. The fact is, a leader can usually afford to take a few hits. Your reputation is already established, and the loyalty and trust you win by shouldering someone else's responsibility far outweighs any damage.

Finally, a leader needs the humility to acknowledge his blind spots. At GP, they called me "Hurricane James," and the nickname followed me to Medtronic. It was mostly a compliment, but it had a little bite. My winds of change blew hard and fast, and every so often they left destruction in their wake. For example, Hurricane James sometimes moved so fast that we failed to ask all the right people the right questions to prepare ourselves. Some of my biggest early successes were followed by some of my biggest failures, as a result. I have been very thankful for the times that employees trusted me enough to point out oversights before we got started and stood their ground those times I tried to blow right past. That, combined with increased discipline around holding risk assessment sessions with, well, everybody, has saved me from uprooting more than a few trees and houses over the years.

By definition, blind spots can only be pointed out by others. A leader needs to encourage others, particularly subordinates, to have the courage to speak up when they see blind spots. If you don't ask people to be proactive, they're likely not to say anything, at least not to your face. Once they do bring a blind spot to your attention, listen and learn. If you think they might be off base, ask a couple other folks. Nine times out of 10, you'll find they were right on the money. Find a way to solve the problem—with their help. In doing so, you're not only improving your leadership ability, you're also creating a more trusting relationship.

As you lead change, there will be challenges that knock you off balance, times when things are breaking so fast that you see the despair in team members' faces and feel that you've let them down. At that point, it will be trust that saves you. Trust that no matter how bad things are, you'll be able to lead the team back on track. Trust that you'll do everything it takes.

Even more important, you'll need trust in yourself to push past self-doubt that will inevitably flare up. The greater the positive difference a change initiative will make, especially a transformational one, the more moments of doubt a leader will have.

The next and final part of the book covers what a leader needs to do to persevere and press on.

*Chapter 9 in Tweets*

- To build trust with bosses and colleagues, forget golf: Help them accomplish their professional priorities.

- To change others, first be willing to change yourself. Step outside your boundaries.

- Teams trust you when you listen, acknowledge them personally, and talk to them straight.

- Put your pride to the side to give others credit and exposure.

- The mark of a true leader is how many other leaders he or she creates.

## Coaching Moments

All "no" answers need to be addressed.

| Question | Answer (Yes or No) |
| --- | --- |
| **1.** Do you know what your boss' and peers' top priorities are for the year, and are you helping them achieve those priorities? | |
| **2.** In the past 12 months, have you supported a hub, financially or through your influence, in achieving his or her goal? | |
| **3.** In the past year, have you stepped outside of your comfort zone (boundary) to engage others? | |

| Question | Answer (Yes or No) |
| --- | --- |
| **4.** Has at least one of the people you have sponsored or are currently sponsoring gone on to a higher position within or outside the company? | |
| **5.** Do you know what your blind spots are, and have you put people in place to prevent you from crashing? | |
| **6.** Do you have a method to deal with self-doubt when it threatens your ability to lead? | |

# Part IV
# Perseverance

# 10 Put Out Every Fire

C ongratulations on getting to this point in the book. You now have a new approach for setting priorities. You understand how to navigate politics. You've got a grasp on the people.

Now there's just one more thing to prepare for: total disaster. An experienced crisis management person once told me that 75 percent of the planning for most crises can be done in advance, yet hardly anyone he had worked with ever took the time for it. No matter how well you plan and execute, "unknown unknowns" can emerge during or after implementation and create sparks. In IT, for example, we spend hours and hours doing stress testing to make sure a new system has enough capacity to handle heavy loads. And yet, almost without fail, when we launch, the system runs slow. Sometimes it even crashes under loads that we "proved" it could handle. I've been burned more times than I can count.

Practical problems become morale problems as teams tire and frustrations rise. These become the defining moments of your leadership. A fire is either quickly snuffed out, or it engulfs the entire initiative and you with it.

Hopefully, you've already positioned yourself for success by using the Getting Lost with Confidence Matrix to set expectations. Too many leaders try to campaign for their initiatives by giving key stakeholders—in particular, the people with the power to shut you down before you even get started—a false sense of security. Risk management is a key task in the work plan, one that will be crossed off as "complete" before the actual transformation begins. It's not surprising, then, that people expect a smooth transition. When things go wrong, time gets wasted as people point fingers and go into "CYA" mode.

In addition to using the matrix to set expectations, I recommend worst-case scenario preparation. Here you focus not on causes or issues, but on potential negative outcomes—the website going down, orders being delayed, and so on—and make plans for how you'd handle them. In IT, the most common worst-case scenario is a system crash that affects customers. Generally I have prepared for this with two safeguards that allow us to muscle through. Prior to launch, I boost the size of our front-line customer care team by 25 percent. That way, we can take orders by phone and have plenty of people to talk to customers if the system goes down. Second, I increase inventory in the field by 25 percent so that we can still fill orders if we have production or distribution problems. When bosses have balked at the expense, I simply calculate the potential volume of lost sales and customers if we were only able to process 50 to 75 percent of their orders for a two- to three-week time frame. Suddenly the cost to prepare doesn't seem so great.

## Forming a Crisis Management Team

The first step of forming a crisis management team happens early in the game. You need to define which types of fires should lead immediately to you being notified. Which they are will depend on your industry. In my case, I had a list of five:

1. When an employee was injured while on the job
2. A situation that adversely affected the environment

**3.** A major potential product or service quality issue

**4.** An IT system, supply chain, or manufacturing outage that lasted more than 30 minutes and could have an adverse impact on our customers

**5.** An adverse internal or external regulatory audit report

Once you've developed your list, make sure every single person touching the project knows it by heart. Quick, direct notification allows you to jump into action and assemble the rest of the team.

I come from the school of leadership that says you should immediately form your crisis management team once you are briefed on the situation. The size and makeup of the team depend on the situation, so not all roles can be planned in advance. There are, however, four that are almost always included. First, a human resources (HR) person to help manage the emotional and human impact of the issues at hand. Second, you need someone with domain experience in the situation. For example, if I'm dealing with a supply chain problem, I want our most experienced supply chain person on the team.

Third on the list is a communications person. This person isn't there to spin the situation, but to ensure that information is communicated promptly and accurately. When things break, everyone else on the team will be so focused on fixing the problem that they forget to communicate important information to others. As a result, negative and inaccurate news starts filling the vacuum, which can make a tense situation worse and lead to more things breaking. Without timely updates, it can seem like leadership has lost control.

Finally, your crisis management team needs a project leader. This person will make sure tasks, timing, and accountabilities are identified, understood, and executed. Having someone organize and coordinate the work at this level of detail not only keeps everyone aligned, but it also gives them confidence that the situation is under control.

## Getting in the Trenches

Getting in the trenches means interacting firsthand with the crisis and the people resolving it. I've seen too many situations in which leaders either waited too long to get involved or didn't stay long enough when they did. As a result, they are dependent on second- or third-hand information, which has a very high probability of not being fully correct.

The telephone game—those times when communication passes through a chain of people before arriving in your ear—always distorts the message, and that's even more so the case in times of crisis. For example, when I was the CIO of GP, our data center once went down in the middle of the night. When it wasn't back up by 5:00 A.M., I got on a plane and flew to the site. By the time I arrived three hours later, the data center was back up. I first spoke to the site manager, who was giving me all kinds of technical jargon about what happened and why the backup power didn't kick in. It was all very complicated, and yet nothing he said fully explained what had happened.

I asked him to take me to where the outage started. When I spoke to the employees there, I finally got the simple, clear version of what had happened. They had installed a new server without first checking the LCD display that showed whether there was enough power to run it, which lead to a short circuit. The backup power source was regrettably on the same electrical unit (another whoopsie), so it went out, too. It was simple human error, and now that we understood it, we could make sure it never happened again. If I hadn't gone straight to the source, I never would have known the true cause of the problem or taken the steps to prevent it from recurring. Note that the leader to whom the employees at the data center reported didn't join me in the trenches. He was too tired from being up all night. (We were all up all night.)

When an initiative you're leading derails, it's your job to do everything in your power to get things back on track. Often that means getting involved in areas of the business that aren't normally your responsibility, at least not directly. That was the case once again at Medtronic after we launched the new ERP system. Overall the system worked okay, but the printers at the warehouse were having trouble. Every time they went down, personnel didn't know which items to pack and couldn't print shipping labels. Meanwhile, they were dealing with a learning curve in using the new system. These problems added up to shipments failing to be ready for FedEx, which lead to customers not getting their orders in time. Remember, Medtronic sells medical devices. Late deliveries could put lives at stake.

The warehouse manager and his staff were very good people, but they were at their wits' end. In addition, their bosses were nowhere to be found; they had moonwalked. To make things worse, the operations leader responsible for the warehouse hadn't increased inventory in the field in case we had problems. As you may have already guessed, we hadn't increased customer care staff either.

After two days of FedEx pulling away with not all of the next-day delivery orders on the trucks, I drove down to the warehouse myself, even though no one there reported to me. I noticed two things. First, adding extra workers would help us to catch up during times when the printers were working. And second, we didn't have any backup plan for when we missed the FedEx cutoff.

We solved both problems. When the warehouse got backlogged, my IT staff and I personally went down to the floor to help pack and label boxes. (Our office was less than 15 minutes from the warehouse.) When we still missed the FedEx cutoff, which happened for about a week, we chartered planes for $17,000 a pop and got the deliveries out on time. The warehouse manager did not have the authority to make spot decisions involving that amount of money, but I did. So we made them. Leaders oftentimes are the only ones who have the authority needed to marshal the needed resources. In their absence, people are hamstrung while they wait for approvals.

Thanks to the warehouse, customer care, and my IT team rolling up their sleeves and putting in extra hours, we stopped missing deliveries. And after three weeks, the printers were fixed and everyone began getting more comfortable with the new system. I immediately gave everyone involved spot bonuses that together totaled $225,000—a sum far lower than what a lost customer would have cost the company.

My involvement attracted the notice of two people. Shortly after everything had calmed down, the out-to-lunch operations leader who ran the warehouse told me to stop telling his people what to do. *He* was in charge. I didn't argue. Well, he wasn't in charge for long. Two months later, my boss called me into his office and added operations to my responsibilities, which meant the warehouses, customer care, and their leaders now reported directly to me.

As an aside, during the crisis, I wasn't thinking about my career. I was taking responsibility for a problem that no one else would. But this time and many others, that approach increased my influence and got me promoted. Getting into the trenches can do the same for you, too.

There's one more reason to dive in: It's an ideal time for you to develop the relationships that make you a better leader. Bonds are forged when people come together in times of crisis. You'll also learn a lot about people: who panic and moonwalk; who rise to the occasion; who stay focused; and, who get the job done. It might not surprise you that more senior people moonwalk than front-line ones.

## In Crisis, Don't Ever Make It about You

I've covered the need for timeliness and accuracy in your communications. There's one more way leaders blow it when it comes to messaging during crises: making it about them. Remember the *Deepwater Horizon* oil spill in 2010, among the industry's worst ever?

The CEO had the experience of keeping it real going wrong when he told media that no one was more focused on stopping the spill than he was—because "he'd like his life back." His company's explosion had caused loss of life and would likely cause environmental devastation decades into the future, and where did he focus the story? On himself, as though his temporary discomfort was worth two beans to the rest of us. With just five wrong words, the entire world now doubted whether the company had the integrity to grasp the gravity of the disaster it had caused and get it fixed as fast as humanly possible.

When things go wrong, a leader doesn't get to commiserate. Anything that happens on your watch is your responsibility, and you have to deal with it. In truth, this isn't just a messaging problem. Ego, that infantile part of you that wants to make it all about you, clouds your ability to make good decisions. I think back to that time I stormed into my boss's office, screaming about wanting to sue because of an audit that wrongly called my work into question. In retrospect, it's so clear to me now that anyone, including my boss, would recognize that audit as the final struggle of someone whose ability to lead was in question. But in that moment, my rational mind was squashed under my raging ego. Screaming wasn't going to fix anything, and in fact it set me back.

Of course we all have egos. We need a work-around, and here's what I suggest: Keep your mind focused on the endgame. The best way to save your reputation is to fix what's broken as quickly as possible. Get it fixed and working better than it ever did before, and that will become your legacy. With that thought and integrity as your guide, you'll keep your ego at bay.

And as a final recourse, when you feel the need to make it about *me, me, me,* take 20 minutes to vent with your closest advisors or someone at home. Get it out with the people who know you so well that they'll see it for what it is: a minor temper tantrum that needs to be released so that you can focus on the real work ahead.

## How to Elevate a Discontented Team

Change is hard work, and even the most dedicated, engaged employees get frustrated. Challenges such as longer-than-usual hours and a steep learning curve lead to exhaustion, complaints, and scapegoating, and eventually to lost productivity, mistakes, and formal resistance. As a leader, you've got to be proactive in managing morale. When people's "change muscles" start to tire and people focus more on blame than on doing the work, there are four things that I've found that consistently refocus the team.

### Address the Issue Head-on

Make sure that your core team members, especially your HR and communications people, know that you want to hear about any concerns voiced by anyone on the project right away, rather than wait for a real problem to emerge. Discuss the situation with HR and communications first. This will give you the chance to vent any defensiveness so that when you talk to the team, your ego is at rest. If they're going to be frustrated with someone, better that it be you than their colleagues. You can also get their advice on how to handle the situation in a way that both addresses their concerns and keeps the project moving forward.

When you're ready, call a meeting with every single person who touches the project. You want everyone to hear you at the same time. Otherwise, your words might be "interpreted" as they're shared. You might also find that singling out individuals to meet with can lead to an impression that you're playing favorites or assigning blame. When people are already unhappy, they tend to assume the worst when people file into a room and the door closes.

The goal when you meet is to address the issues head-on, but without being confrontational. I've found that when you can, meeting in an informal venue helps. For example, when I enlisted my IT leadership team to work on the warehouse floor during the enterprise resource planning (ERP) crisis, it was not without complaint. After the first day on the floor, I could see that the mood was bitter. We all met for dinner at 10:00 P.M. that night, and after a couple of beers, people were ready to talk. They were frustrated that I was making them do work outside of their responsibilities to make up for the poor leadership at the warehouse, which wasn't their fault. They were carrying the full weight of the start-up problems on their shoulders, even though any number of things could have been done by operations to help. Meanwhile, they needed more time to troubleshoot actual bugs with the new system.

In short, they were tired, losing confidence, and looking for a scapegoat. If I didn't step in, they would become the 4-year-old who screams "that's not fair!" before melting into a tantrum. This is not unusual when things go wrong during an initiative. Here's what I said, and what you can say when you face this kind of situation: "No, it's not fair. Leadership is rarely fair: You are often uncredited for the good, and falsely blamed for the bad. But it doesn't matter, because your job is to solve the problem and save others from pain. Maybe, once you take care of the problem, you can address questions of who did what."

Use this analogy: If we were driving down the street and saw kids lying hurt on the side of the road, our responsibility is to stop and help them, not shake our heads and wonder where their parents are. After they got the help they needed, then we would ask those questions.

You have to find a message that helps your team rise to the occasion. After that night, there was no more grumbling. Several of my VPs started going to the warehouse without me needing to ask.

## Let Them Air Their Concerns, But Keep the Tone Civil

It's important that you sit and listen to the team's concerns. There might well be something actionable that you need to address before you can quiet their rumblings. But you also have to stay in control.

When people are disrespectful, call them on it. If you let people vent without keeping the discussion civil, it can have long-term consequences on relationships and your leadership. The motto of these meetings should be, "We can disagree, but not be disagreeable in the process." Keep your own emotions in check; getting angry is a quick way to lose respect in the eyes of your people.

## Never Pass the Buck

There will be times when you have to make unpopular decisions regarding staffing (layoffs), organizational changes (replacing popular but disruptive leaders), and compensation. When people react badly, you may feel the urge to shift the blame upward: "It wasn't my call" or "It's policy." Squelch that urge. Hearing that their "fearless" leader is someone's lap dog doesn't make anyone feel better, it only makes you less trustworthy. Own every decision you make, and even if people are angry, at least they'll know you're a straight shooter.

When I was an IT director at Georgia-Pacific, I became a hero to my people when I gave them a "Year 2000" bonus—and a goat when I took it away the following year. The bonus had been in response to skyrocketing IT salaries when demand increased thanks to the Y2K bug. Other companies increased salaries and then had to lay people off. We did bonuses so that no one would lose their jobs when the IT market cooled down.

When I heard from my HR leader that a group of employees were planning to protest their case to the CEO, I called a town hall meeting. First I summarized their concerns, and then I told them that I had made the decision. I could have fobbed off responsibility to the CIO, who in fact had made the call organization-wide. But the fact was, I supported the decision and would have made it myself. It was the right call. I laid out the logic, which was based on three different salary studies. Then I let people know that we'd be watching the market; if it picked back up, I would make sure we stayed competitive.

After that meeting, the noise died down. People still didn't like the decision, but they had accepted it as fair. The fact was they trusted me. If they had heard the same message from the more-removed CIO, or if I had passed the buck, they might have continued to protest or started searching actively for other offers. Both would have been bad for the company and for me. And ultimately, it would have been bad for them, because our compensation was competitive, and I gave them ample opportunities to grow their careers within GP.

## Deal with Malcontents One-on-One

Many times your efforts will succeed with all but a handful of people. Sometimes those folks just won't quit, and they can stir people back up once you've settled them down. That's what happened with the bonus issue. A single employee kept up her campaign, and her behavior grew increasingly toxic. She was spending her work hours sowing discontent instead of doing work. She was the type of person who talked to everybody, usually to gossip, and therefore she had a certain amount of social influence.

In such cases, don't waste the group's time on a second meeting. At this point it's a personal problem, not an organizational one. I called this woman to my office and let her know that I was aware of her behavior. I repeated the reasoning behind our decision, and I let her know that appeals to the rest of the executive team would meet deaf ears—we were all aligned. I also let her know that I could see she had real influence. And here she was wasting an opportunity to show the organization that she could lead.

Dealing with me one-on-one, she quickly backpedalled and tried to implicate others as the troublemakers. After that meeting, I never heard another word. When it comes to true malcontents, divide and conquer. They rarely have the truth or integrity on their side, and they back down easily when asked to take responsibility for their actions.

## Step into Your Power

When disasters happen, you may have moments where you feel that keeping things under control is hopeless. Even the best planning, leadership, and people can't stop problems from happening. In fact, those aren't crazy thoughts: You're seeing the world as it is. You can't control everything. So be it. Push aside your despair, because in those times when things are out of control you have to remember what you do have: The power of true and trusted leadership to move hearts and minds. It's not insignificant, and it can rescue you from even the worst disasters.

I didn't fully realize the extent of that power until I faced something I hope none of you ever have to: a death on site. At the time, I was the vice president of GP's Distribution Division's mid-Atlantic and southeast regions. I got a call around 2:00 P.M. that a warehouseman in North Carolina had been fatally hit by one of our 18-wheeler trucks right outside the entrance to the property.

Following the advice of my HR colleague, we both immediately got on a plane. His role would be to work with the person's family, organize grief counseling for his colleagues, and prepare me for what I should expect on site. As for me, I wasn't totally sure what I was going to do; I just felt deeply that being there in person mattered.

I didn't know how right I was. When we arrived at the warehouse at the end of the workday, it was completely full of employees. Everyone from the first shift, when the accident had happened, had stayed, and all of the second shift employees had joined them. The grief in the room was overwhelming. Heads were hanging and many people were crying. When we arrived, all eyes turned to me, searching for something.

I looked around at the room, taking it all in, and then spoke from the heart. I told them that while I didn't know the man personally, I wished I did because it was clear from the grief in everyone's faces that this had been a very special man who went out of his way to help others. When I saw people's heads nodding, I knew what to do next. I asked if anyone wanted to share with the group how the man had helped him or her.

As people spoke, the crushing sense of grief started to dissipate. People were still sad, but they were moving beyond the state of shock and helplessness that we found them in. I closed by letting them know we were going next to his family, to take care of them. We also let them know that grief counselors were available to all. When I closed my remarks, more than one person came up to hug me and say thank you. Later that week we attended his funeral services, among the most touching I have ever participated in.

It wasn't until that day on the floor that I understood how desperately people need leaders in times of crisis. I had never seen myself as someone whose mere presence could provide emotional support and start to renew people's sense of safety, significance, and control. Now I recognized that while VP was just a title, there was incredible power in the leadership opportunity it presented if I stepped up to it both in crisis and in moments of celebration as well.

Crisis mints leaders, forcing them to stand up and stand out. Learn all you can from the challenges. You may as well, because you can be sure they'll keep coming.

## Chapter 10 in Tweets

- The best change leaders identify and prepare for worst-case scenarios.
- Does your team know which kinds of crises should lead to a direct call to you? If not, make the list now.

*(continued)*

*(continued)*

- Seventy-five percent of crisis planning can be done before the crisis. Be the rare leader who does it.
- When things go wrong, a leader doesn't get to commiserate. Your watch, your responsibility.
- Own every decision you make. Even if people are angry, at least they'll know you shoot straight.

## Coaching Moments

All "no" answers need to be addressed.

| Question | Answer (Yes or No) |
|---|---|
| **1.** Are crisis management teams and plans in place, and have you drilled them in the past 12 months? | |
| **2.** Do your direct reports know which scenarios should result in you being immediately notified? | |
| **3.** Did you deal with the last major fire in person, on the ground? | |
| **4.** In the past, when the team felt dissatisfied with leadership or a particular situation, do people feel that you addressed the situation head-on and took accountability for your decisions? (Have your HR person ask people this question so that you will receive candid feedback.) | |
| **5.** Do you have sponsors and mentors you can open up to when facing challenges—and have you done so in the past 12 months? | |

# 11 Institutionalize and Leverage Change

I magine this scenario: Two companies implement the same IT system. They use the same vendors to manage the project and implement the changes. They use the same outsourcing and contract manufacturing companies. And yet, they achieve very different results. Five years out, company A has seen incredible, direct benefits from the change. Company B is struggling, hindered by the same problems the system was supposed to fix.

I've seen this happen many times, and the question becomes, how could two companies that implemented similar changes get such different results?

The answer often ends up being fairly straightforward: Company B changed the infrastructure but never changed the culture by making needed changes to processes, behaviors, organization charts, decision-making authority, and so on. Even small holdovers of the old ways can eat away at gains. For example, the ERP system we implemented at Medtronic made real-time information accessible to all. But we couldn't reap the benefits of that until we had also increased the decision-making authority of front-line people so that they could act on what they learned. Processes had to change, too. The system allowed us to increase the use of automated orders, at least in theory. But I sat down with a representative in our customer care group one day and found out that all those electronic orders were being manually reviewed before being released to the warehouse, eating up all the efficiency the streamlined system was intended to create.

## Why Organizations Lose Their Focus

To catch and follow through on all the changes, an organization needs long-term focus and real cultural change. Let's start by talking about the reasons why organizations lose their focus.

### Short-Term Financial Distraction

CEOs and boards have to balance the need to achieve short-term quarterly earnings against the demands of long-term strategic initiatives. If they don't do it well, the budget and man hours devoted to change initiatives are gutted to meet immediate financial priorities, and the longer-term, higher-value rewards never come to fruition.

This is nothing new. Experienced change agents manage expenses to protect their initiative from this threat. Budget for the best, but plan for the worst. "The worst" in this case is when management asks you to reduce the initiative's cost by 10 or 15 percent in order to meet Wall Street's quarterly earnings expectations. Not meeting expectations can result in a serious drop in stock price. If it happens several times, Wall Street and large shareholders start questioning the effectiveness of the company's leadership, and heads roll.

When asked to reduce costs, be prepared; otherwise your boss can legitimately question how supportive you are to the overall success of the organization and not just the change initiative you are leading.

The best way to pave the way for cost reductions that won't adversely impact the initiative is by making sure at least 25 percent of the resources working on it are contract employees rather than full-time employees. Reserve full-time staff for the most critical aspects of the initiative. With this kind of flexibility in the team, you can pull back as needed without shutting the project down. If you're working with a third party to bring in contractors, you'll need a strategic relationship to get past the normal stipulation of 60 to 90 days' notice before reducing employee numbers. That's not enough flexibility to reduce cost before the end of a quarter. By building a solid, forward-looking relationship, I've been successful in negotiating 15- and 30-day notice periods. That's a staffing model that provides the flexibility you need to support the company while maintaining the initiative's momentum.

## Change Overload

Another reason why change isn't sustained is that there are too many changes taking place at once. It reminds me of the lyrics in one of my favorite songs, which I'll paraphrase: *I can't do what 10 people tell me, so I guess I won't change.* People can only focus their attention on a few things at once. If there are too many "top priorities," people will fall back on doing things the way they know. In other words, if everything is important, nothing is. A close relative of change overload is "change de jour," when organizations pile on a new top priority annually before the previous ones have been implemented. People never fully engage because they know that something new is right around the corner.

To prevent overload from occurring, I have a "rule of three." At any one time, my teams had three top strategic priorities, and each person had three individual priorities directly linked to the strategic priorities. The same goes for operational and tactical priorities. They don't change unless something material, like an acquisition or major quality issue, comes up.

## Leadership Transitions

It takes a good three to seven years to institutionalize change, especially transformational change. Trouble is, most senior executives don't stay in their positions that long, and there's no guarantee that new leadership will support your initiative. There are a couple of ways to protect yourself against this risk. One is to be on the watch for your boss's likely successor and start cultivating that relationship early. The other is to cultivate relationships across the executive level so that you have a strong base of support that can help to influence a new leader on the scene. For most large-scale change, you're lost without the support of the CEO, whose influence reaches beyond every functional barrier.

When I was interviewing with Medtronic, the CEO was more than five years into his tenure. Meanwhile, realizing the full benefits of the ERP system implementation at the center of my mandate would take five to seven years. As a result, I rested my decision on my evaluation of his successor more than on my evaluation of him. Medtronic made it easy for me because, at that time, they had a very orderly CEO succession process. When they named the CEO, they normally named the COO at the same time. When the CEO retired, the COO would succeed him, and the process would repeat itself.

When interviewing with the COO, I asked enough questions to be sure that he supported implementing the ERP system, and not just because it was the politically correct thing to do as long as the current CEO was around.

I didn't stop there. I also evaluated the next most important and influential person in the company: the CFO, who was positioned to be there for a while. I was relieved to find he was the ERP system's most enthusiastic supporter. Since he had been with Medtronic for over 15 years, he also knew what the challenges would be in implementing it, especially in IT, which had been reporting to him while the company completed its CIO search. The CFO turned out to be a great business partner and trusted friend.

I knew that the challenge at Medtronic would be great, and I didn't want to take it on if I didn't believe it could be successful. All change agents need to make that kind of evaluation when considering a new campaign. If evidence mounts that success is unlikely in your current environment, you're better off taking your ambitions elsewhere.

## Continued Resistance

Even years into an initiative, those people who fought you, in particular the Machiavellis, will continue to resurface. They'll take action any time there's a business challenge that can be linked, however remotely, to the change you achieved. At this later stage in the game, they have a whole new set of tactics. Here's what to watch for and how to persevere.

- **The money pit:** The instigator exaggerates the costs of the initiative and underestimates the benefits, arguing that to continue would be throwing good money after bad. This is when having the CFO as your partner saves you. His numbers are the ones the top brass listen to.

- **The revisionist history:** This tactic, used by a lot of people who were firefighters in the old culture, involves spreading a revisionist history of the organization prior to the change, at which time things were "so much better." They have either conveniently forgotten about or minimized the big fire that was the catalyst for change in the first place. Don't try to address this yourself; your version of history, however accurate, will be seen as biased and self-serving. Instead, punt this one once more to the CFO. He or she has the numbers and the high-level perspective to remind people how bad things really were.

- **The chicken dance:** Chicken Littles want to convince everyone the sky is falling, and the only way to save the organization is to roll back to the old ways. They're relentless in trying to represent every growing pain as the sign of a metastasizing cancer. As when facing political challenges in the past, an independent third-party audit is your friend. Be careful with consulting firms, because they have their own reasons to diagnose a cancer: They then can sell themselves as the cure. Whenever possible, start instead with your internal audit department. Taking this approach often has a secondary benefit. Generally the head of internal audit reports to the audit committee of the company's board of directors. He will be in executive session with them and will speak to the initiative's progress (or lack thereof). Asking for an independent review will let you see in advance what he will be saying. You do have to be ready to take the good with the bad and the ugly—but change leaders should always welcome independent, unbiased feedback.

The bottom line is, you always need to be prepared for challenges. You'll be at a business review, and someone will show that he won't be able to meet his numbers for the quarter (or worse yet, for the year) because of problems associated with the change initiative. All eyes will then turn to you for some type of response. The worst possible answer is, "I'll look into it and get back to you." That answer makes you look out of control and oblivious to the impact of your work.

Ideally, you want to be able to say that you have been directly involved, you have taken steps (which you outline), and to put the cherry on it all, you already have an independent assessment underway. But to be able to give such a response, you'll need to go into every meeting prepared for anything, armed with facts. Keep nurturing relationships with your hubs!

## Evolving the Culture

Earlier in the chapter on messaging, I talked about the need to speak to the culture of the organization you're trying to change. Meeting them where they are eases the transition to new behaviors and values, and all the practical changes that follow—to processes, organizational charts, changed responsibilities, and so on.

But in order to make change stick, leaders must proactively help the culture evolve so that they preserve what's important from the "old way" but also find purchase for the new way. To be truly successful, you need employees to do more than follow the new processes and behaviors by the book. If that's all you achieve, then as soon as the "book" gets buried, people roll back to old behaviors. What you really need is for employees to understand the new mission so well that they help you rewrite the book going forward. That's where culture comes into play.

For example, in my earlier example about the ERP system helping to automate orders at Medtronic, there were two cultural values in play. First, there was the need to offer our customers top quality—a founding value of the company. But we also needed employees to embrace a new value, frugality, so that we could meet customers' expectations and stay competitive. We had introduced a technology that would allow for both efficiency and quality in the ordering process, but only if employees understood why it was important and trusted the technology to automate some functions. Training played a big roll in that shift, but we also needed to help the culture evolve by pulling on the same three levers I mentioned before: language, celebrations, and heroes.

The ABCs of a common business language are metrics, which executives use to communicate with each other and throughout the company. That saying "What gets measured gets done" should be broadened to "What gets measured gets done *and* communicated." Metrics are key to changing the culture and institutionalizing change. The cost side is usually straightforward: Tightened budgets and increased attention to them emphasize the need to focus on efficiency. To make sure that we maintained quality at the same time, we developed new metrics around customer satisfaction and error-free regulatory inspections.

To further enshrine quality amidst the changes, we created new awards for "highest quality" and "most improved" among the business units. The CEO presented these personally on an annual basis. We also started celebrating successful regulatory reviews, instituted an annual event in which R&D teams showcased their experiences using the new methodology, and started having quarterly quality reviews with executive management in which the CEO and all of the business unit GMs and EVPs participated. The VPs—the same ones who at the outset were so convinced that shared standards were impossible—helped lead the reviews. Of course they did: They had become the heroes who made the transformation happen.

We needed heroes that embodied cost-effectiveness, too. Ed Bakken himself made a huge contribution there. At Medtronic's annual holiday party, the company's biggest celebration, Ed took time in his opening comments to praise the work I was doing. For the company's hero innovator to acknowledge someone who was leading efficiency and effectiveness change initiatives was a seminal moment. Nothing is more powerful than a current hero lending his support to a new one.

### A Small but Powerful Tool for Change

When colleagues become partners in or exemplars of the change you're leading, there's a powerful but often overlooked way to keep them energized: a thoughtful, handwritten thank-you note. People have sent me e-mails with the images of thank-you notes I had written them 10 years prior. When you thank someone via e-mail, the note is often buried in a person's memory as soon as it is buried in his or her inbox. Handwritten notes, few and far between these days, often take up residence on a desk, bulletin board, or drawer, increasing their impact. Individual thank-you notes of any kind are much more powerful than group notes. The more specific they are about the person's effort, the more powerful.

## Making Metrics Matter

Developing metrics is one thing. Getting people to work hard over time to improve their achievement against them is another. You can create banners, screen savers, and LCD signs displaying the metrics, but they don't do much. To see the numbers improve, people need to be held individually accountable and incented. By doing so, you are investing every single employee in the success of the initiative.

Just like earnings, metrics need to be reviewed quarterly by executive management to stay front and center over time. During the transformation at Medtronic, the CEO used his quarterly town hall meetings, which were broadcast to the organization worldwide, to share how we were doing against our new metrics.

He celebrated successes, but when a business unit had a quarter with poor results, he called it out in front of everyone. Given the "hometown pride" of each business unit, that kind of public shame made meaningful impact.

The CEO's public support for the new metrics is essential, particularly in situations when new metrics and their corresponding priorities are competing with the old culture. For example, when we had start-up problems after the ERP implementation, the CEO and other top executives never questioned that we were taking the right step forward, even as the business units were looking to shut us down.

If you're having trouble getting the CEO on board, huddle with the CFO and the head of human resources for help. If together you can't change his or her mind, start planning your exit. The chances that your initiative will take root are next to zero.

## The Power of Documentation

The power of common, accurate documentation to keep an evolving organization on course cannot be underestimated. It resolves disputes and prevents misunderstandings. Everyone should be working off the same version and should be able to follow the history and authorship of changes. In addition, they should be able to quickly chat and caucus when there are questions or misunderstandings.

Common documentation is also powerful when it comes to training. Indeed, effectively and efficiently training people around the world on new processes, policies, and people has been a persistent challenge for change agents in global organizations. In the past, we hired technical writers who created many volumes of binders filled with training and policy information. Many a tree lost its life for the cause. Unfortunately, those documents were outdated by the time they were printed, and they were rarely at hand when people actually needed them.

Today, technology offers many solutions to make documentation flexible, accessible, and searchable. When training, I recommend online "best practices" wikis or forums. Within them, people can post questions they have about new technology, processes, and so on and have their peers answer them. For example, an employee might need to know how to execute a certain transaction within the new system. These forums can include "cheat sheets" or FAQs that address the most frequent challenges faced as people navigate the new way of doing things.

These forums, available to all, do more than improve information flow and sustain change. They also bring people together across functions and around the world. Everyone from the CEO to a warehouse worker can post on them. As a result, mental boundaries start to expand, and the sense of having a shared culture expands. While an HR or other community leader might monitor the forums to help surface the best information and ensure accuracy, it's vital that information be able to move freely from the bottom up.

## To Leverage Change, Keep Tearing Down Walls

In the aftermath of a successful initiative, you have a unique opportunity. People's minds have been forced open, their boundaries ripped down or rewritten. Now is the time to leverage that state of being by looking proactively for the next big transformation. If you don't find it, you can bet it will find you—in a less-than-ideal state of preparedness.

Look for those barriers that are interrupting or slowing the four flows of business: Information, products and services, money, and people. If you can take down those barriers, you will be rewarded with more efficiency and better solutions.

### Information

To maximize the benefits of change, remove barriers to the flow of information first; those changes make it possible to address all the others. That's why I always initially focused my attention on the IT systems. A sage mentor once told me, "The quickest way to tell how customer-focused and effective an organization is this: count its customer databases." In other words, when data is tucked into multiple databases, it's exceedingly difficult for any one person to have a 360-degree view of the customer. When I arrived, Medtronic had more than 16 ERP systems. Consolidating and reconciling data took a tremendous amount of time, and frequently we'd find people's numbers didn't match. "Truth" was dependent on which system you were using, both in terms of the actual numbers and how they were interpreted.

Only once we reached critical mass with the ERP implementation were we ready to turn our attention to tearing down other walls, at which point the benefits became more and more substantial. We consolidated the data centers and IT systems and flattened our IT and operations organizations. We removed over 20 vice president, senior director, and director positions. With information flowing freely, we were able to turn front-line and middle management into decision makers instead of just policy administrators, communicators, and problem escalators. The impact was profound. We lowered our year-over-year actual cost for seven years in a row, even as our volume increased by over 100 percent as a result of the company's growth. Our effectiveness (quality) also improved based on our customer satisfaction results. Any time we came in under budget, I put the funds toward innovation and quality improvements within the business units—the aforementioned "Dallas Dollars."

Beyond the ERP implementation, we found other ways to improve the flow of information. We upgraded and extended our telecommunications network to customers, suppliers, and, most importantly, each other. As a result, we increased collaboration by making it easier and faster for people to connect with each other. We worked with R&D to create "innovation" campaigns. Within them, we posed questions and problems not only to our R&D personnel around the world, but also to people outside of the company.

## Products and Services

Once a common IT and communications infrastructure is implemented, the next place to start looking for barriers is in the supply chain, for products companies. Specifically, look to see how many warehouses (distribution centers) there are throughout the company. Here's why: Once you have a common IT system that gives everyone real-time visibility of customer demand, supply, and manufacturing, you can start replacing inventory with information.

In other words, you can start synchronizing your supply chain with your customers and suppliers. For example, Medtronic had more than 13 distribution centers in the United States and seven in Puerto Rico, our largest manufacturing site at the time. After consolidation, we had four in total, as well as an improved rate of on-time delivery.

For service companies, the parallel barriers are those related to transaction processing—orders, invoices, payments, service requests, and so on. A good place to start is service requests, since they are the most important ones to the customers. For example, if service requests have to be manually initiated by the customer (a wall), figure out a way to integrate your IT system with theirs so that the process is automated. If that isn't possible, focus on making the process as easy as possible for customers. For example, hotels and rental car companies these days are working hard to simplify the reservation and checkout processes.

*Ease* is the key word for improving flow of both products and services. The next priority is *scale* because it allows you to grow while keeping your incremental cost low.

## Money

At Medtronic, as at other product companies, the flow of money starts with a customer placing his or her order. It ends with payment and the closing of books at the time of quarterly and annual financial statements. Moving to a single ERP system allows us to start automating transactions; before, the system was too complex. We went from automating 5 percent of transactions to 70 percent—figures that represent a huge barrier being removed in terms of the customer's ability to move quickly and easily through the purchase process. Money flowed while customer satisfaction shot up from an average score of around 3 to more than 4 on a scale of 1 to 5 (1 was the worst). The time it took to close the books went from weeks to days. Finally, we were able to cut days off of our cash flow by automating the flow of transactions.

Automated transactions, e-commerce, and electronic payment options are all examples of ways that companies remove barriers to the flow of money. The technologies not only speed up payments by removing paper mail, but they also improve accuracy. Prices are checked and compared in advance of invoicing and payment.

## People

Changing how people interact with each other and the company may be the single most powerful opportunity for change. You see people flows are interrupted when functions or divisions are siloed, when stratified hierarchies narrowly circumscribe behavior and contributions, and when physical walls or distance stifle collaboration.

When people get comfortable and start trusting each other, boundaries fall and change is leveraged most effectively. New ideas bubble and surface. At Medtronic, the big breakthrough in our quality transformation occurred when the R&D, manufacturing, and quality leaders across the entire organization collaborated on the design for an initiative focused on taking quality to the next level given the increasing complexity of our new products. For the first time ever, the functions came together, rather than R&D taking the lead and involving quality and manufacturing later on in the process. As a result, less iteration was required before and after products were launched. It was a better way to work.

Shifting to cross-functional collaboration required both mind-set changes and infrastructural upgrades. People had to rebuild their belief systems around how things "should" get done to much more collaborative models. Meanwhile, moving to a common IT and telecommunications system allowed people around the world to work from common documentation and communicate with ease.

As people interact more frequently and with a more diverse group, build on each other's ideas, and are empowered to resolve problems on their own, employee engagement also increases, which again propels new benefits. I've never seen my IT teams more energized than when working hand-in-hand with customers, suppliers, and other internal functions such as marketing, engineering, and sales.

Energized teams, in the end, are what you need more than anything to sustain change—and then to continue evolving, finding every opportunity to help your company do more of what it does, and better. In a rapidly changing world, you'll be most successful when it's not just you coming up with the billion-dollar ideas, but the people who work for you. That's the true art of change leadership, and the work never ends.

### *Chapter 11 in Tweets*

- To succeed in changing your organization, get the support of your CEO or bust.
- Flexible employment contracts help change initiatives stay afloat during short-term budget squeezes.
- New metrics institutionalize change—if every individual is measured and rewarded.
- To sustain change, change the culture. To change the culture, change the metrics, the heroes, and the celebrations.
- Documentation is the change agent's friend. Make it accessible, flexible, and open to all.

*(continued)*

*(continued)*

- To leverage change, keep changing. Remove barriers to the flow of information, then move on to products, money, and people.

- A handwritten thank-you note is a powerful tool for agents of change.

## Coaching Moments

All "no" answers need to be addressed.

| Question | Answer (Yes or No) |
| --- | --- |
| **1.** If the change has been implemented for longer than six months, have you had an independent third party do an assessment? | |
| **2.** Are common metrics being monitored by executive management? Are the people who achieve them being celebrated, and are those who fail being held accountable? | |
| **3.** If the change initiative is more than a year old, is the organization still giving it enough focus to bring its full, long-term benefits to fruition? | |
| **4.** Have you created or utilized an existing online forum for sharing best practices? | |
| **5.** Have you identified and started working on the next change initiative, one that will allow you to more fully leverage the prior one? | |

# 12 Developing Talent as a Sponsor

Leaders who are invested in change must also invest in talent. You should be constantly on the lookout for future leaders to groom and position for success in the organization. And at any given time, you should have several people in mind who are on track to be qualified and ready to replace you when you move up or out of the organization.

In my experience, formal leadership development programs are too superficial to prepare employees to shoulder the challenges of change. They generally offer some type of personality assessment and feature lectures by professors or authors. Really lucky "high-potential employees" might find themselves on an international trip. Such a trip might be good for retention, but doesn't do much in the way of training. Overall, formal leadership development is too academic, and can't be relied on to develop the experience and grit that are needed to succeed in any position of significant responsibility.

My own approach to developing talent, I will admit, requires a significant investment of your own time and energy. But the returns are great, providing the best means of sustaining and leveraging change. On top of that, there is a multiplier effect, because your approach with those who you sponsor will influence their approach with others. It's satisfying when you realize that by investing in one person, you're in fact impacting many.

I recommend that change leaders focus their effort on sponsorship rather than mentorship. In my definition, mentors are chosen by the student, whereas sponsors pick their "sponsees." Sponsorship is strategic: You are focusing on people who you believe deserve to rise high in the organization, and who can help both your short-term and your long-term initiatives succeed. You want to be close enough to them that you can be hands-on, offering both coaching and opportunities that will push them to develop. If they're not already in your group, the first step is to get them transitioned or promoted so that they're within the reach of your authority, where you can have real impact.

The strategy behind sponsorship doesn't mean that these relationships aren't generous. They're extremely generous. You could say that I mentor all those whom I sponsor. You are investing in their success as much as in yours or the organization's. You have to be, in order for the relationship to be successful. To help them grow, you have to get to know the whole person—and in many cases, that means their family, too. With that level of relationship, personal investment comes naturally. If it doesn't, you've almost certainly chosen the wrong person.

## Whom to Sponsor?

There are many qualities that suggest a propensity for leadership. Over time, I've settled on five that I find are specifically indicative of someone who is up to the pressure and unique challenges of leading change, and therefore worthy of sponsorship. Here's what to look for. Not everyone will have all five qualities, but you'll help them develop the areas in which they fall short.

**nce:** I actually prefer to call resilience "the ability to look tains." I list this one first because it is far and away the most . Looking over mountains requires character, courage, and creativity. Has the person stood up during tough times, overcome obstacles, or taken accountability for a plan to improve?

On the ground during a business crisis is the best time to identify the most resilient in your company. Who provides direction and boosts morale? Who takes a stand and doesn't budge when second-guessed? Frequently the people who show resilience in such moments are not the ones I would have chosen from the day-to-day crowd, or who would have been cherry-picked for formal leadership development.

When we had the reporting crisis after the launch of the enterprise resource planning (ERP) system at Medtronic, most people didn't look over the mountain; they slammed right into it. There was a lot of yelling, and much time was wasted pointing fingers. We were all surprised when a soft-spoken middle manager from the accounting department stood up in a meeting and outlined the exact steps we needed to take to allow the business to close its books. Everyone listened like she was Warren Buffett. I knew immediately that I wanted to bring her into my group. Two years later, she was a VP running our global customer care operation. Despite not having the background for the position, she did an outstanding job thanks to her ability to see over mountains and get her team to climb them.

**Authenticity:** Otherwise known as "straight shooters," authentic people engender trust. People unfortunately have the tendency to think that the higher up they go in an organization the more buttoned-up they have to be, making it seem like they're always in control.

I was once on the selection committee to choose a new senior leader. One of our top contenders was outstanding on paper, but in person she was falling short. A number of the committee members saw her as too buttoned-up. She was so professional that she seemed to be hiding her true self. They questioned whether she could be trusted to be transparent as challenges inevitably arose.

I personally believed that the problem was with her presentation, not her integrity. So I met with her myself and shared the group's reservations. If she wanted the job, she needed to relax, let down her guard, and be herself in her next interviews. She heard what I said and after her next round of interviews, everyone felt much more comfortable. She ultimately won the position, and these days is first and foremost known for being a straight shooter.

There's a second reason why authenticity is key. You can't effectively coach a person who isn't willing to share his or her true emotions and thoughts with you, both the highs and the lows. You won't know when you're needed or how to help, and even if you did, the individual would be unlikely to hear your advice. Unwillingness to open up and admit weakness is one of the top things that I see holding back otherwise impressive young professionals. It's a mind-set that "protects" them from a lot of much-needed learning.

**Inclusiveness:** Find people who seek multiple perspectives, and see the value in all kinds of diversity. Those who don't are showing that they prefer the status quo and will never proactively seek a better way of doing things, no matter how much you coach them. Watch carefully who emerging leaders put on their teams. I once declined to do business with an offshore services company because it didn't have a single female in management. That sent a negative message to our own female managers, and made me question whether an outfit with such a limited purview would provide the best solutions.

Inclusive people also have the ability to cross boundaries and build bridges between them, both of which are essential to the success of transformational change and acquisition integration initiatives. The most inclusive leader I ever worked with was Bill Hawkins, a former CEO of Medtronic. He built teams of very diverse leaders and constantly sought our input. We respected him more, not less, for relying on our counsel, and no person was better suited to position Medtronic for future success.

**Inquisitiveness:** Inquisitive people constantly engage others. They are always asking questions: *How are you doing? Why do they do it that way? What do you think about this? What changes do we need to make? How are our customers doing?*

An enthusiasm for asking questions suggests strong leadership potential. First, it shows that the questioners are always in learning mode and don't care who does the teaching. Second, asking questions is a practice that helps make the people they interact with feel significant and respected. And third, it shows that they are comfortable with saying, "I don't know, but I will find out." This trait is essential to finding your way with confidence after you get lost. Question askers are generally in the habit of asking for advice before making decisions. They don't waste valuable time trying to figure everything out on their own, or let their pride get in the way of changing their position when compelling information or ideas are presented.

**Inclination to develop others:** The fifth and last trait to look for is the person's inclination to develop others. I'm not going to invest in anyone who has an "it's all about me and if it weren't for me" attitude. People with that mentality aren't going to build effective teams. In fact, they view very capable people as a threat and will actively undermine them. Meanwhile, those who are generous with their knowledge, time, and influence are the ones who will turn your investment into a real growth portfolio.

To recognize this trait, watch how the person introduces you to colleagues or direct reports. You want to hear things like "This person is an up-and-coming star" or "If it weren't for her, we wouldn't have been successful." Watch how they interact with others. Do they collaborate and delegate? If they are already managers, do they coach and mentor their direct reports?

I have at times seen people whose egos inflate once they have been given extra responsibility and power. I can empathize to some extent. I remember that when I first became an officer at Georgia-Pacific, I felt like I'd gone to bed James Dallas and woken up Denzel Washington. Well, it only took one "you'd better check yourself" look from my wife to bring me back down to earth.

That said, I have seen people who never recovered from that initial leap in self-importance. They let the power and status go to their heads, and suddenly all their decisions become focused on protecting their position instead of doing good work or doing right. Time and time again, I've found that those who show an early inclination to develop others rarely suffer from this pitfall. As they rise, they pull others up with them.

## Awaken New Leaders

Once I've identified someone I think I'd like to sponsor, my work with them begins with a conversation. I sit them down and tell them the number one reason I've chosen them: their ability to see over mountains. This insight seems to surprise them all. Either they didn't see themselves that way or they didn't realize anybody else did. I make sure that they leave the room with the understanding that this trait suggests a tremendous ability to make a much greater difference than most people, inside the organization and out.

I call this initial conversation "the awakening," and I recommend that you have one like it with anyone you are sponsoring. The goal is to build their confidence and, if necessary, help them take the leap to seeing themselves as leaders. Because professional culture is still strongly affected by gender bias, I have found that women need help shifting their mind-set more often than men. (I take pride in the number of females I have sponsored who are now in executive positions in Fortune 500 companies.) My experience is that women are more likely than men to be concerned about a knowledge gap when offered a new opportunity. Some women are also more hesitant to speak up or speak again when they aren't heard or get shot down.

To further awaken leaders, encourage them to think back to times they have led others through difficult challenges, whether in their professional or in their personal life. As they share these stories, they begin to see themselves and interpret their experiences in a new light. You can see it in their faces and body language. They start to believe that they *do* have a special ability to see over mountains and lead others to climb them, and it sets them apart from the rest. This positions them to accept and even request challenges and responsibilities that require them to step into new territory.

Occasionally you might sponsor people who are starting with the opposite problem: overconfidence. They overcommit and overpromise. With this group, encourage them to be more thoughtful and measured before making commitments.

Once we've worked on confidence, I give sponsees a task list of three other things they'll need to work on to be successful as change leaders:

1. Defining a higher purpose for their work. With that level of per-spective buoying them, they will find the courage to put themselves at risk for the sake of others. They will stand up and offer solutions when others shrink into the corner.

2. Developing a strong personal brand, one that compels people to speak positively about them when they are not in the room and to support them when they are.

3. Finding a theme song that they play that picks them up when they have either fallen or been knocked down.

You probably think I'm joking about the third item. I'm not! I'm very serious. As change leaders, I tell them, there will be times in which your intentions are misunderstood, times in which you will be blamed for things you didn't do, times in which you won't get credit for things you did do, times in which people will let you down, and times in which you'll find you've made an honest but mortifying mistake. During those lows, you need some way of picking yourself up.

I have two theme songs: "Back in Stride Again" by the R&B group Frankie Beverly and Maze, and "Back in Black" by the hard rock group AC/DC.

## Develop Their Personal Brand

Developing a strong personal brand requires some perspective, which you can provide. In fact, without the perspective of a trustworthy second party, it's pretty much impossible. Your help starts informally, by helping them reconceive their past experiences—both highs and lows—as leadership assets, stories that they can use to let people know who they are, what they value, and who they value. With these stories in their pocket, they'll never give speeches; instead, they'll share experiences that translate into purpose and forward momentum for the people listening.

Formal training really helps jump their presentation to the next level. Every person I sponsor spends time with a professional communications coach. The coach makes sure that their authenticity is evident when they are talking to others. The coach films them talking and provides candid, direct feedback.

As a next step in developing their brand, find out how they are perceived by others. Typically this is done by engaging a formal 360-degree review or other outside assessment. However, I recommend a simpler approach that I've found is much more effective: Set meetings between you and the most influential or senior people they've worked with to ask how they've been perceived so far.

These meetings serve three purposes. First, you'll get valuable information about qualities that the person needs to improve upon. Second, you're building their reputation already by letting others know that you've taken a professional interest in their success. And third, it allows you to form closer relationships with the individuals whose opinions you're seeking.

Once you've taken those meetings, you can work with the person to develop a plan to change how they are perceived. Sometimes that means working on changing behaviors or developing new skills or habits. For example, in my own case, a sponsor once told me that the way I sat made it seem like I wasn't listening or taking seriously whomever I was speaking to. I was surprised by the feedback, and not sure whether I believed it was a problem until I saw a video of myself. Then I immediately knew he was right: I was leaning back in my chair, arms crossed, with my legs sprawled out in front of me. You might have thought that I was heading into a nap, but meanwhile I was conducting business! I realized that this was a habit I had developed years back when I had my knee surgery, when keeping my legs straight kept the pain level manageable. As soon as I saw myself through my sponsor's eyes, I developed the habit of sitting up and leaning forward when listening to others, and immediately sensed a positive response.

Other times, improving your sponsees' brand might require you to step in and influence the way they are perceived by others. Find opportunities to call out their overlooked qualities to other senior leaders. For example, earlier I mentioned the soft-spoken woman in accounting who went on to become a VP in my group. Because she was so soft-spoken, people assumed she had nothing to contribute and tended to ignore her when she did speak. I started telling people that she, unlike most people, never spoke just for the sake of being heard. And when she did say something, you'd better listen closely because you could be sure it would be spot-on.

There's one more step to helping sponsees improve their personal brand: Help them protect themselves from their blind spots. Blind spots are different from developmental needs. The latter can be addressed through training, both formal and informal. Blind spots, on the other hand, are resistant to training because by definition the leader isn't aware of them until the moment that something or someone else brings them to his or her attention.

The way I coach people to deal with blind spots is first to let them know any I've noticed myself. Then I suggest that they select three people they trust and ask them to keep a lookout for those behaviors, and any other blind spots they see. Such trusted advisors are essential to leaders, especially as they move up the ladder. You need people who "speak truth to power"—telling you when you're about to shoot yourself in the foot—and the easiest way to make sure you have them is to deputize them in advance.

## Put Them in the Hot Seat

A good sponsor provides opportunities for exposure to and interaction with executive management. Whenever possible, let your protégés give the updates to higher-ups, instead of you doing all of the talking. Defer decisions to them, and include them in as many meeting as you can with influentials in the company. In those meetings, help them put their best foot forward by steering their contributions, particularly if they're rambling or struggling to make their point. For example, you might say something like "It may be helpful if you talked about the XX situation as an example," or "Tell them about the increase in sales we have seen from customer YY."

Including them in meetings isn't enough. You also need to give them real opportunities to develop their change leadership capabilities. The fastest, most effective way to do that is trial by fire: putting them in positions of responsibility even when they don't have the functional expertise—but making clear that you're there to support them and won't let them fail.

People may question your actions, and urge you to go with more seasoned functional experts. To get support for an unorthodox choice, acknowledge the holes but then pivot the conversation toward what makes you believe they are capable of the job. For example, when I put the accountant in charge of global customer care, people didn't know what to think. I pointed out that while in accounting she had developed tremendous respect among the field sales leaders and that she was great at streamlining processes. Since our goal was to improve our support to our field sales force and streamline the customer service process, she was actually a great choice. Honestly, they were still skeptical, but they gave her the benefit of the doubt. Time proved that she was the right person for the job.

Once you put your charges in these stretch roles, you'll find out quickly whether they need to work on yet another vital trait of successful change leaders: asking early and often for advice. If you don't see them doing this, it's time for another conversation. I've personally found that at least 50 percent of the times I have either fallen or been knocked down could have been prevented if I had reached up and gotten the advice of more senior people before I took action. I make sure that those I sponsor head into their new responsibilities with that lesson in mind.

## When Sponsorship Fails

My approach to developing emerging leaders is a very hands-on process. It requires significant time and commitment on the part of the change leader. Because it's such a huge undertaking, it's important to make sure you're working with people who are deserving and capable of your investment. Even when you've chosen the people you'll sponsor carefully, you sometimes find along the way they weren't ready or able to shine in the way you'd hoped.

I have a fairly straightforward way of deciding when to end a sponsorship. If I give advice three times in a row and it is ignored, for whatever reason, it is clear that we're on different paths. I tell them directly that our relationship is no longer serving them. They need to find a sponsor who they feel gives advice worth taking.

If things are working well, timely, direct, and honest feedback and advice are some of the most important benefits you offer sponsees. Of course, they won't always agree, which is what you'd expect when dealing with someone who has initiative and ideas. Push them to back up their point of view with considered arguments and maybe you'll even learn something yourself. However, there will be times when sponsees stop listening because they think they have nothing to learn, or because their decision-making process has collapsed to a single question: "What's best for me?"

Sometimes as a sponsee moves up the ladder, increasing self-importance leads to a change in leadership style. For example, I once promoted a young woman and significantly broadened her responsibility by making her the manager of the group. Within a couple of months, I noticed that collaboration and morale were really hurting. People weren't interacting with each other comfortably, and fewer people were visiting my office. I couldn't figure it out, until one day I came back unusually early from lunch. As I turned the corner to my office, I found her sitting in my chair and berating one of her employees. I was shocked. She quickly tried to pass it off as them using my office to have a private conversation. The look on her employee's face told me everything I needed to know. My sponsee had turned into a tyrant, and was using my sponsorship to terrorize the team. She was removed from her position the next day, and the group returned to normal.

## Provide Air Cover for Risk Taking

Providing your protégés with air cover is critical. They need to feel safe to lead in new functional areas, and to try new approaches—their earliest experiments with leading change. One of my most memorable moments occurred when a man I was sponsoring was attacked in an e-mail by a senior leader for proactively reaching out to customers to ask how we could serve them better. The recipient (we'll call him

Mark) was devastated, and forwarded the e-mail to me asking for my advice. I didn't see anything wrong with Mark's interaction with customers—in fact, I thought it was just what a change leader should do.

I immediately recognized the attack e-mail, which was far from professional in tone, as a power play. The leader was threatened by Mark's expanding role, and had more confidence than he should have because his own sponsor had a lot of influence in the company. I forwarded the e-mail to his sponsor, and noted that it violated every core value of the company.

Immediately after I hit the send key, I got a call from his sponsor, apologizing for the guy's behavior. Soon thereafter, Mark and I both got calls from the e-mail writer, apologizing. From that point on, he was very supportive of Mark because he knew that I had his back.

Another time, a sponsee had successfully completed a proof of concept (POC) that promised to improve customer satisfaction significantly. She came to me with the idea, the POC results, and the business and country sponsor. Now she needed investment to scale the initiative. Because the amount of funding she needed was more than my approval limit, we had to go to the CFO and CEO. They both said yes, with the caveat that my organization couldn't go over budget for the year. "No problem," I said, knowing full well that we didn't actually have the room in our existing budget—yet. I knew we could find it.

When the finance VP for our group later questioned where the money would come from, I smiled widely at my sponsee's response: "That's something we'll figure out later. Let's focus on making sure that we successfully implement the initiative." I couldn't have said it better myself. And sure enough, we finished the year within our budget.

In another situation, a leader had an idea for how to reduce significantly the cost of operating our facilities. I was very impressed by how she took on the risk of making it happen. When the vendor she chose proved to be a weak partner, I was so proud of the way she took accountability and, more important, developed an alternative plan. When people tried to be critical of her and the initiative in meetings, I came to her defense. I pointed out that the plan was sound, but the vendor didn't deliver. She was the one who ultimately saved the situation, however, by coming up with a plan B that resulted in cost reductions in the millions of dollars.

Providing air cover gives your sponsees the space they need to lean into new opportunities without fear of damaging their careers. To become capable change leaders, they need, quite simply, to have had the chance to screw up and then fix it, with your help if they need it. On the other side of the coin, when they succeed, you should be the first to make sure everyone in the organization knows it. I had a sponsee who developed an innovation center that was funded by the suppliers whose products it showcased. Everything about the initiative won my admiration: the unique funding source, the diverse team of mavericks he put together to develop it, and the way he stood firm when people questioned why was it being built and whether it was outside the scope of his responsibility. When it turned out to be a huge success, people tried to give me the credit for building it. I made it very clear that it was his idea and his victory.

You don't need any credit. Sponsoring others is its own reward. And in the long-term, you'll find that being generous with your expertise and sharing the spotlight will serve your career much, much more than being known for solving all the big problems yourself.

## Coaching Moments

Use the following checklist to identify and develop emerging talent. Each question should be graded on a scale of 1 to 3, with 3 being the best. You and your sponsee should work together toward the highest ratings across the board.

| Question | Rating (from 1 to 3) |
|---|---|
| 1. Has the person demonstrated a "getting lost with confidence" mind-set? | |
| 2. Does the person communicate with authenticity? | |
| 3. Has the person created a strong personal brand that is recognized by colleagues of all levels? | |
| 4. Does the person know his or her blind spots and have people watching to prevent him or her from crashing? | |
| 5. Is the person getting exposure to executive management? | |
| 6. Does the person seek out and seriously consider advice? | |
| 7. Is the person building an inclusive team and sponsoring others? | |
| 8. Is the person proactive in finding opportunities to initiate and lead change? | |

# EPILOGUE

**M**ost of this book has been focused on looking outward to find ways to improve your organization and then collaborating with others to make change happen. However, I want to leave you with the recommendation that, at some point, each of you look *inward* to advance your leadership goals and deepen your impact.

During the first decades of my career, my goals were straightforward. Having grown up in a family with meager finances, I was constantly working to build a better life for my wife and me, and eventually for our daughter. I was doing some community work and I always took time to assist colleagues in need, but I never thought a great deal about whether my work should have a purpose beyond creating financial ease for my family.

That changed in 2000, when I attended a team-building program called "Leaders Developing Leaders." I almost didn't go because my experience with professional development off-sites up until that point had left me skeptical. Spending a day catching blindfolded teammates while they fell backward wasn't, in my opinion, the best way to build trust. But after I sent three of my people and they came back raving, I decided I should try it.

The program was based on Noel Tichy's book *The Leadership Engine.* Tichy's central idea is that the number one role of a leader is to develop other leaders. To do that well, he says that everyone needs a "teachable point of view" that guides his or her mentorship of others. To develop our unique POVs, the facilitators had us develop a "journey line" that listed the most significant highs and lows of our lives. Among my lows were the death of my grandmother and major knee surgery that left me in casts and then braces for a full six months. Among my highs were marrying my wife, watching her achieve her lifelong dream of becoming a nurse, bringing my first major professional initiative to successful fruition, the promotions of my protégés, watching a 10-year-old-kid that I mentored go from introverted to confident. ... As I reviewed the list, I started to notice a theme. All of my highs happened when I was serving a purpose greater than myself, usually helping someone else to be successful.

You then had to review your journey line with the rest of the participants. Never before had I talked about my personal history in front of a group of business colleagues. Sharing my stories and hearing those of others was the most powerful trust-building, boundary-expanding professional experience I've had.

As I thought more about where I had come from and where I had arrived, my teachable point of view became, "To make a difference, you have to be willing to be different." In other words, you have to be willing to throw yourself at new experiences and new environments to broaden your understanding, perspective, network, and influence. It's a leadership philosophy that, put into practice even before I had articulated it, prepared me well to navigate through change with intelligence and drive and to teach others to do the same.

Later, I developed a personal mission statement as well: "to encourage and enable people who are trying to make a positive difference in their lives and in the lives of others." I began to consciously seek out people who needed help, opening their minds and opening doors for them. I'm very proud that, today, I can count more than 30 individuals at senior levels in Fortune 500 companies who would say that I played an important role in their development.

Becoming conscious of my true purpose fundamentally changed the ways I spent my time. Before, I spent 80 percent of it on tasks

20 percent on relationships and service to others, and hardly any on my own personal development. Afterward, I reversed it to spend 20 percent on tasks, 70 percent on relationships, and 10 percent on myself.

I mention this now because I do wish that I had taken these steps earlier in my career. In the years since, I've seen that many leaders get so caught in the daily churn that they stop investing in other people and themselves. They stop taking time to learn. And finally, they lose sight of their North Star, or worst yet, never take the time to identify one. Knowing my higher purpose made it easier to stay focused and strong when my projects ran into challenges and when my leadership was called into question—most of all by me. It increased my commitment, allowing me to achieve more and feel better about it when every day was done.

So having done all you can to figure out *how* to make change happen, I encourage all of you to think also about *why* you do it. Find the answer, and you're truly ready to lead your teams toward the greatest success.

# ABOUT THE AUTHOR

H. James Dallas is an accomplished senior executive with extensive experience as an agent of change in large domestic and international corporate settings. He has successfully implemented over 10 transformational and turnaround initiatives, 20 acquisition integrations, 5 operations/quality shared services centers of excellence, and 3 innovation centers. Mr. Dallas has over 30 years of experience in general management/business operations roles as well as chief information officer positions. He retired in September 2013 as senior vice president of quality, operations, and IT at Medtronic, Inc., a global medical technology company that employs approximately 45,000 people and does business in more than 120 countries. He also served as a member of Medtronic's executive management team. Prior to joining Medtronic in 2006, Mr. Dallas was vice president and chief information officer at Georgia-Pacific Corporation, a global forest products company that employs over 55,000 people. In his 22 years at Georgia-Pacific, Mr. Dallas held a series of progressively more responsible information technology and operating roles. He also served as a member of Georgia-Pacific's executive management team. The majority of his career has been focused on bridging the gap between strategy and execution, using IT both strategically and entrepreneurially, and leadership development. Mr. Dallas serves on the boards of for-profit and nonprofit organizations. He has been named one of the most powerful black men in corporate America several times in his career by *Black Enterprise* and *Savoy* magazines. Mr. Dallas is a native of Atlanta, Georgia. He and his wife Celest have been married for 34 years and have three daughters.

## Links to James Dallas's Website and Videos

- Website: www.jdallasassociates.com
- Video: https://playback.service.emory.edu/ess/portal/section/
  637dd7e9-2638-4fa1-827a-e66688c38396
- SAS webcasts: www.sas.com/research
- YouTube video: http://youtu.be/O8NeYG1jagA

# INDEX